BRUCE LEE and I

An Intimate Portrait by Bruce Lee's Training Partner
and the Father of Taekwondo in The United States

GRANDMASTER
JHOON RHEE
FOREWORD BY LINDA LEE CADWELL

MVM Books
Fairfax, Virginia

Publisher's Cataloging-in-Publication
(Provided by Quality Books, Inc.)

Rhee, Jhoon.
    Bruce Lee and I / Jhoon Rhee. – 1st ed.
    p. cm.
    Includes bibliographical references and index.

1. Lee, Bruce, 1940-1973—Juvenile literature.
    2. Rhee, Jhoon--Juvenile literature. 3. Martial artists--
    United States—Biography--Juvenile literature.
    I. Title.

PN2287.L2897R44 2000   791.43'028'092
    QBI00-745

ISBN 1-931135-00-2

Published in the United States by
Multimedia Vertical Markets, Inc.
MVM Books
4200 Lafayette Center Drive, Suite A
Chantilly, VA 20151

Manufactured in the United States of America

10 9 8 7 6 5 4 3 2 1

Designed by Boldface Design

First Edition

Books are available in quantity for promotional or premium use. Write to Director, MVM Books, 4200 Lafayette Center Drive, Suite A, Chantilly, VA 20151, for information on discounts and terms or call (703) 263-9505.

Other Books by Jhoon Rhee

Chon-Ji of Tae Kwon Do Hyung

Tan-Gun and To-San of Tae Kwon Do Hyung

Won-Kyu and Yul-Kok of Tae Kwon Do Hyung

Chung-Gun and Toi Gye of Tae Kwon Do Hyung

Hwa-Rang and Chung-Mu of Tae Kwon Do Hyung

Character for Champions (by Charles Sutherland and Jhoon Rhee)

Acknowledgment

For a first generation Korean-American to write any book in English is not a simple task. Fortunately, I had a few friends who helped out.

They are: Bob Atkins, Linda Cadwell, Tom Callos, Ken Carlson John Corcoran, Christopher Cubbage, Nancy Hansen, Marina Kim, Sam Lindsey, Earle Martin, Ben MacLachlan, Al Santoli, Steven Taylor, and the team at Boldface Design, Inc.

I would like to make a special acknowledgment to Jonathan Slevin, whose hard work and commitment to excellence have enabled me to honor the memory of Bruce Lee and, I believe, also fulfill the high expectations of his legions of admirers worldwide, who have waited many years for me to complete this task.

Dedication

I would like to dedicate this book to America's Founding Fathers—George Washington, George Mason, Benjamin Franklin, Thomas Jefferson, and many others—who affected the quality of life for all mankind by establishing a Freedom System for the first time in history. They laid the foundation for a society and world where everyone can be happy with every breath of life.

I also dedicate this book to:

My late parents, Jin Hoon and Kay Im Rhee, who with great sacrifice raised their five children with emphasis on our moral and character education, during a time of terrible living standards in Korea.

My late wife, Han Soon, who was with me for 30 years of happy life and brought four beautiful children into this world. They are: Joanne, Jimmy, Chun, and Me Me.

My wife, Theresa, whose unselfish dedication to others provides me with a constant source of inspiration.

Bruce Lee and Linda Lee Cadwell, for all they have done for Martial Arts worldwide and for me, personally. Through this book, I have sought in some small way to honor the remarkable legacy of excellence in mind and body that Bruce left behind in his too short life.

Jhoon Rhee

BRUCE LEE and I

An Intimate Portrait by Bruce Lee's Training Partner
and the Father of Taekwondo in The United States

GRANDMASTER
JHOON RHEE

FOREWORD BY LINDA LEE CADWELL

Contents

Foreword

Linda Lee Cadwell

*"you will gain insights into the
lives of both of these extraordinary
men by reading the memorable
stories of a long and trusted friendship"*
—Linda Lee Cadwell

It is a great honor for me to write an introductory note to Master
Jhoon Rhee's book, *Bruce Lee and I*. My late husband, Bruce Lee,
was a great friend and colleague of Master Rhee for more than a
decade, from 1964 until Bruce died in 1973. During that time they
carried on a continuous discussion about the martial arts, both on
technical points and philosophical principles.

Bruce and I were frequent houseguests of Master Rhee and his gracious late wife, Han Soon. On these occasions, Bruce and Jhoon
would talk and practice techniques late into the night. Bruce
attended the Jhoon Rhee Nationals every year from 1966 to 1970,
and the two of us even gave a demonstration at the 1970 tournament. Master Rhee often visited our home in California, and when

Master Rhee came to Hong Kong in 1973 for the filming of his movie, "When Tae Kwon Do Strikes, " the two of them were together on almost a daily basis. I have many fond memories of the times our family spent with Master Rhee and his family. And along the way Bruce and I developed an enduring taste for Korean food.

Bruce Lee had great respect and admiration for Master Jhoon Rhee. They shared this mutual respect because their work expresses an intense passion for the martial arts as a way of life. Bruce was inspired by Master Rhee's dedication to learning, the purity of his motives, and the discipline of his training. Bruce and I often talked about how Jhoon Rhee was a man who acted, not just talked, and who could turn his visions into reality. He has proven his ability to do this by his many accomplishments—from teaching martial artists how to make a good living through effective management, to conducting seminars on living a healthy and happy life.

Bruce Lee would be very proud of the success of his friend Jhoon Rhee. I think you will gain insights into the lives of both of these extraordinary men by reading the memorable stories of a long and trusted friendship in Grandmaster Rhee's book, *Bruce Lee and I.*

I wish you all
> great health,
>> abundant energy
>>> and quiet awareness,

Linda Lee Cadwell

Introduction

Thank You Bruce Lee

"...think of electrons darting around the nucleus of an atom. That is the speed at which the great, late martial artist Bruce Lee could move his hands."
—*Jhoon Rhee*

Think of the fastest cheetah on the African tundra. Think of the speed at which you blink your eyes. Or better yet, think of electrons darting around the nucleus of an atom. That is the speed at which the great, late martial artist Bruce Lee could move his hands. When I first saw Bruce demonstrate his punches, I subconsciously thought of many things that are lightning-fast, including the velocity of atomic particles—perhaps because of my training as an engineer. Those hands helped make the man.

But, of course, so too does the mind, heart and spirit make the man. Bruce was blessed with a clear and thoughtful mind, a kind and generous heart and a rich and playful spirit. Bruce Lee was one of my best friends, and I feel fortunate to have known him and to have shared many wonderful experiences with him. I wish that all of you who are reading this could meet Bruce. But of course that is impossible because, as you know, he died tragically and prematurely in 1973.

During our friendship in the late 1960s and early 1970s, Bruce wrote me many personal letters. They shed new light on this man whose popularity has grown posthumously. Bruce was a passionate reader, and he became a very good writer. His wife, Linda Lee Cadwell, recently told me that Bruce's love of reading led him to writing. "He always felt a need to record his thoughts," she said. "Of course in the days before all of our new communications technology, letter-writing was quite an art form. And, Bruce became a prolific letter writer. He did it partly for the recipient of the letters and partly for him, as he loved to put his thoughts into words—and lucky for all of us because we now have a pretty good record of much of what he was thinking and doing."

Yes, Linda, we are lucky. I am especially fortunate because I have kept the letters Bruce wrote to me—19 in all. One day a few years ago, I read through all those letters and was struck—as I often am when remembering my friend—by Bruce's vast mental capacity and treasured and cultivated personal philosophy. When I re-read them a few years ago, I felt guilty that I had been hoarding them away, however unintentionally, from the public. I decided to publish these letters in the form of a book to share his personality and winning philosophy with all his admirers around the world. But you know, until about 15 years ago, I didn't even keep these letters in a safe. I just thought of them as a very special friend's correspondence. But my son, Chun, told me to put them in a safe. "These are treasured letters, Dad," he told me. "Do you know how precious they are now and how much more valuable they'll become as time goes by? Take care of them." He was right, of course, because, while Bruce may have written a lot, not many people still have his letters. My collection has since come to be referred to as "The Jhoon Rhee Letters."

In this book, I also want to share some of my memories of Bruce, his spirit, life and career. While many of Bruce's fans may know much about his life, I think I may be able to offer another perspective—certainly one that is grounded in respect and fondness—partially because of my own experience in taekwondo. That is, I can appreciate the degree of dedication it takes to become a master in the martial arts, and I fully understand the commitment Bruce made to his craft.

A Lesson in Friendship

Furthermore, I hope this book expresses, through Bruce's examples, a lot about the nature of friendship. When I recently read through all his correspondence with me, I started thinking that maybe I had taken for granted how much he had done for me over the years of our close friendship. He had also done so much for his other friends. In the 1960s, for example, he was always helping his friends by promoting them, and their activities, to Mito Uyehara, the publisher of *Black Belt* magazine. It was Bruce who persuaded Mito to publish my five books on taekwondo through his book publishing company, Ohara Publications. On many occasions, Bruce also talked Mito into publishing articles about my taekwondo activities in both *Black Belt* and *Karate Illustrated* magazines.

I openly admit that I forgot how nice Bruce had been to me and how much he had done for me in so many ways during those early years of martial arts in the United States. He even came up with the idea of me doing a movie. I remember he called one day—out of the blue—and said, "Hey Jhoon, I think you should do a taekwondo movie. I'll arrange it. Would you be interested?" I said, "Of course, I'd be interested." So he introduced me to Raymond Chow, his partner and the chairman of Golden Harvest, a film company, and I soon found myself playing a lead role in a Hong Kong feature-length motion picture, "The Sting of the Dragon Master" (a.k.a., "When Taekwondo Strikes"). Now I knew that, unlike Bruce, I am not movie star material because I was never chosen to play a role in a high school drama, not even the smallest part. Nevertheless, because of my friend, I "lit up the silver screen," as they say, for one shining moment—my 15 minutes of cinematic fame, to paraphrase the late pop artist Andy Warhol.

Bruce also helped me promote the taekwondo championship tournaments that I orchestrated and that, I've been told, have done so much to launch this form of martial arts out to the American public. From 1967 through 1970, he came every year to my Washington, D.C. tournaments. You must remember that at that time the television series "The Green Hornet" was a popular show in which, of course, Bruce played the character Kato, which meant he was getting more famous every day.

So, we were able to tell the public that Kato is coming to the tournament, and many people would come just to see him. We could advertise it this way: "Jhoon Rhee National Championships with an appearance by Bruce Lee." When he'd come, *The Washington Post* would send out a reporter and interview him. That was the most visible way that people would learn about the championships. The newspaper coverage added credibility to the events. I had a friend who was a reporter at the *Post*, the late Jim Bethea. He was a very good writer and fully appreciated the martial arts but needed a good reason to cover the tournament. Bruce Lee was a very good reason and he gave his time, and his heart, because he believed in taekwondo. I am still very grateful because people flocked to the events.

When I recently spoke to Linda, who sometimes would accompany Bruce to the tournaments, she summarized the impact her husband had. "The audience was curious to know if this Kato character was really a martial artist or if it was all for show, for the TV series," she said. "Of course they would find out that he was very much for real. He gave such electric demonstrations that there was no doubt that he was a truly talented martial artist."

During the Washington events, Bruce would stay at my house. We'd take advantage of the time to have fun together. Like a couple of misbehaving teenagers, we'd stay up late—way past our bedtimes! We'd talk until three or four in the morning about all kinds of things but mostly martial arts and our philosophies. We'd be dressed in sweat pants and t-shirts so that we could practice our kicks, punches and jumps. And we would eat and eat. Bruce liked sushi, especially seaweed-wrapped rice. So my wife would make plates and plates of it and we'd eat all night— talking, jabbing and blocking in between bites of sushi.

The funny thing is, we'd do all of this in the living room, which meant we'd have to move the coffee table and other furniture out of the way and make a big space. Sometimes my wife complained to me that we were making too much noise. They were never ugly complaints and she'd never let Bruce hear her because she liked him and didn't want to offend him. But she'd say privately to me, "Jhoon, please try to be quiet so that your family can sleep." I suppose we were quite loud but we were just being friends—no doubt, rambunctious friends.

The times we had around the tournament are very fond memories for me—almost more memorable than the events themselves. But at one of the tournaments, a particular incident really stands out in my mind. Bruce and his wife Linda performed quite a stunt, one which really brought the house down with uproarious laughter and thunderous applause. As far as I know, it's never before been told in print. And, in this book, I think I'll let Linda tell it herself ... but not now; I'm getting ahead of myself. Instead, let me describe the first time Bruce and I met.

The Mutual Admiration Society

On a hot sultry August 2 in 1964, I met Bruce Lee for the first time at the late Grandmaster Ed Parker's International Karate Championships in Long Beach, California. I was a 32-year-old "young" man and Bruce was just 23 but looked about 16 years old. We were both invited to perform our respective demonstrations between the fighting matches. Bruce showed off his rapid-fire punching abilities, and that's when my mind conjured up the image of hyperactive electrons zipping around the nucleus of an atom. I was also very impressed by other aspects of Bruce's presentations, particularly his close-quarter hand techniques while blindfolded. I was never trained in this and I remember my jaw just dropping to the floor when I saw him perform without the benefit of sight. To be honest with you though, his kicks didn't impress me then.

For my part, I gave a front jump-kick demonstration, breaking three one-inch-thick boards held at seven feet in the air. It was one of my two demo trademarks back then. The other was performing a triple side-jump kick in the air before landing back on the floor. Bruce was impressed by my presentation just as I was with his. He said, "Your kick is very powerful" and he called it a "thing of beauty." Needless to say, I complimented him on his punching techniques as well. (A few years later, we traded our expertise. That is, he taught me how to use my hands and I taught him how to get the most out of his legs.) In the evening, after our demos, we spent an hour or so sharing our martial arts experiences. At that time, to him, martial arts was his life. To me, taekwondo was my life.

We didn't see each other or speak for another year and a half.

Then, one morning in the spring of 1966, I was watching a television show on Channel 7 in Washington, D.C., that showed Bruce promoting "The Green Hornet." In this interview, Bruce was extremely witty and verbally skillful. In person, he had a way of making people feel comfortable and, I discovered, this talent transferred well over the TV airwaves. "You know, Bruce had a charisma and a magical way of communicating with an audience, whether he was before a live audience, a movie audience or viewers at home watching TV," Linda told me. She's right.

After the show, I called the television station. I knew people there, and asked for Bruce. Someone was kind enough to let me talk to him. I asked to meet with him and he invited me to have lunch with him in one hour at the Washington Shoreham Hotel where he was staying. I accepted his invitation and met him in his luxury suite at the hotel. Bruce appeared to be a little cocky and arrogant, yet very warm and funny. I liked Bruce's humor, and I enjoyed his company very much. That's when I invited him as my special guest of honor to my National Championships in May 1966. He cordially accepted the invitation.

"Bruce did these demos at your tournaments because he valued your friendship, Jhoon," Linda told me. "He wouldn't go to just any old martial arts tournament. He was quite in demand at that time and he did a lot of traveling on publicity tours for "The Green Hornet" show, so it was not his favorite thing to be jetting all around. But he'd go anywhere if he could help you, Jhoon."

From the time we ate lunch at the Shoreham until he died—and I spoke to him the day before he died—Bruce Lee and I were wonderful friends who bonded together through our passionate devotion to the martial arts.

Chapter One

Bruce's Early Years;
In and Out of Trouble

*"A good instructor functions as a
pointer of the truth, exposing the
student's vulnerability, forcing him to
explore himself both internally and
externally, and finally integrating
himself with his being*[1].*"*
—Bruce Lee

I think it's important for me to recount in my own words Bruce's
early life—before he met me. I have read a number of biographies
of him, talked to Linda, his friends and others with whom he had
talked about his upbringing. And, of course, from time to time
Bruce himself would tell me about his childhood. I believe I can
add much to the biographic record of this extraordinary man.

Bruce Lee was born in San Francisco on November 27, 1940, the
Year of the Dragon, in the Hour of the Dragon (between 6 and 8
a.m.). His Chinese name was Lee Jun Fan, which means "return
again," because his mother thought her son might come back to

---

[1]Linda Lee, The Bruce Lee Story, Ohara Publications, Burbank, Calif., 1989, p. 22.

the United States to live someday. Bruce's father, Lee Hoi Chuen, was famous in Hong Kong as a comic stage personality with the Cantonese Opera Company of Hong Kong. This explains in part where Bruce got his fantastic sense of humor, and why, years later, he was able to make me and his close friends and family roll on the floor in laughter.

Bruce was born while his father was on tour, performing in various Chinatowns across the United States. But then the Lees returned to their home in the Kowloon section of Hong Kong in early 1941. They lived in a small flat with an extended family of close to 20 people. As I think about this—the crowded household that surely teemed with high-volume commotion—I wonder if this is why later on in life Bruce cultivated only a few friendships rather than dozens of acquaintance-relationships. He declined to become a big player on the Hollywood party circuit and instead sought serenity and order in his life. He'd had enough chaos at home in Kowloon!

Bruce's father was handsome and had a strong stage presence, both qualities, of course, that Bruce inherited. He loved and respected his father. He told me that he did not have as much time with his father as he would have liked, since the elder Lee was often away on tour. However, whenever he could, Bruce's father would bring his son backstage from a very early age, and young Bruce was captivated by the lights, sounds and pageantry of the theater. He once told me—half in jest—that he was a screen star

2

before he was weaned. Come to think of it, maybe he wasn't joking all that much. That is, Bruce actually had his first part in a movie when he was only three months old; he appeared in a scene in a Chinese movie being shot in San Francisco. Bruce considered his real cinematic start, however, a film called "The Beginning of a Boy," in which he appeared at the ripe old age of six. Bruce loved the movie business, and was far more enthusiastic about acting than attending school. By the time he was 18, he had appeared in 20 films. In his final movie as a child actor, "The Orphan," he was truly the star, playing the role of a juvenile delinquent. That strikes me as humorously ironic because the adult Bruce—as I knew him in real life, not reel life —was such an upstanding citizen. I can't even imagine him being a deviant of any sort.

3

The other side of Bruce's life is more confused and contradictory, according to both Linda and his biographers. His childhood took place against the backdrop of the Japanese occupation of China during World War II and the Communist victory over mainland China. After the Japanese were forced out, the hated British occupation returned. There were very few avenues of escape for the slum-dwellers of Hong Kong. As Bruce once said, "Kids there have nothing to look forward to. The white kids (British) have all the best jobs and the rest of us had to work for them. That's why most of the kids become punks. Life in Hong Kong is so bad. Kids in slums can never get out[2]." Bruce wound

---

[2]Lee, p. 26.

up seeking out the gang life, which wasn't hard to find. Again, this is so paradoxical to the Bruce I knew as an adult.

A lackluster student, Bruce rejected the rote methods his instructors used to teach academic subjects, just as later in life he would reject traditional methods of teaching martial arts. From an early age, he had exhibited the powerful energy and charisma that would eventually make him a sought-after teacher and then an adult star. Bruce threw himself into the violent street culture. Yet when he was 12, he began to attend a Catholic academy, LaSalle College, in which the classes were taught in English. Here again, Bruce belonged to a gang, and eventually, he would be expelled from La Salle for low grades, and for his incorrigible need to fight.

4

The Young Bruce Needed "Joy of Discipline"

I wish that the young Bruce could have had the opportunity to participate in something like my own character education programs which I've conducted with elementary school children since the early 1980s. Please allow me to digress from Bruce's early-years biography to explain my "Joy of Discipline" Program because I feel it is one of the most important aspects of my life as a teacher. With good instruction, children learn the self-discipline and mutual respect that's inherent in taekwondo. They also develop a deep reserve of knowledge. As they grow up and become leaders, they help us maintain our strength and integrity as a nation.

Through the good offices of Mr. William Bennett, U.S. Secretary of Education during President Reagan's first term, I was able to introduce my ideas into a couple of Washington, D.C.-area elementary schools as a test project. Ken Carlson, my dear friend and former student, has subsequently led the development of the "Joy of Discipline" Program into elementary public schools in Virginia, and I have taken it to Moscow and Ukraine. For several years, after teaching morning sessions of taekwondo to members of the U.S. Congress in the Rayburn House gymnasium, I went to schools twice weekly to instruct children from first-grade through sixth in my form of martial arts. I call these sessions, "attitude classes," because attitude is an integral part of the martial arts, as it is in any other worthy endeavor. I teach the kids "chario," or attention, and "kyungye," respect. Students must recite four daily affirmations, which helps them build their inner strength.

5

The affirmations are:

- **I am wise because I always learn something good every day. (Knowledge in the mind)**
- **I am humanly perfect because I never make mistakes knowingly. (Honesty in the heart)**
- **I like myself because I always take action to make good things happen. (Strength in the body)**
- **I am happy that I am me because I always choose to be happy. (Everything happens for the best)**

The martial arts offer a profound method to integrate the workings of our mind and body. If we can instruct our young children how to pay undivided attention and hold a sense of respect for teachers, they can better realize their potential, and be much less likely to hurt themselves or others. In lieu of the recent school shootings, from Springfield, Oregon to Columbine High in Colorado, something has become very clear: We need to help our young people in every way we can. I think the solution to crime and other social ills of our society depends on establishing good families, good role models and character education.

Our "Joy of Discipline" Program is making a difference. Teachers and principals have told me about children who have changed their approach to life after participating in my program. (See "Joy of Discipline" Program in the Appendix.) For example, a boy in a suburban Washington grade school who had developed a reputation for being a bully walked away from a fight because he had learned about self-discipline and individual respect. The principal who told me of this boy's transformation, credited "The Joy of Discipline" Program. A fourth-grade girl in a Virginia elementary school told the entire student body at an assembly how she felt much safer after the Joy of Discipline program taught her to walk away from conflict with confidence.

Another principal told *Washington Post* columnist William Raspberry this: "I thought the children would be so eager to show off what they learned that they would be hurting each other on the playground." She was happily proved wrong. The 45 or so students from that school who enrolled in my program became the least likely among their peers to get in trouble. Raspberry attended one of my sessions and came away surprised as well. "To tell the truth," he wrote in a 1990 column called 'Change Young Lives and Change the World,' "I have come expecting to see a bunch of fledgling fighters put through their paces by their world-famous teacher. I am expecting a six- or seven-year-old's version of a blood-curdling battle cry, a few heel-of-the-hand blows to some vital spot (punches pulled, of course) and a take-down or two...I expect action. What I get is philosophy[3]."

Enter the Honorable Yip Man

But let's get back to Bruce. Shortly after he began at La Salle College, as an early teenager, he realized he needed to back up his bravado; Bruce was the type of person who would tell people exactly what he thought of them. And it wasn't always complimentary. One day Bruce asked his mother if he could be trained in self-defense. He had occasionally joined his father to practice Mr. Lee's beloved tai-chi chuan, but the slow motion and routine nature of the movements bored and frustrated Bruce. His mother decided to hire a teacher for her son, and that is how Yip Man entered Bruce's life.

Yip Man, a master of the Wing Chun branch of kung-fu, had a decisive influence on Bruce's development. He introduced the

---

[3]William Raspberry, "Change Young Lives and Change the World," The Washington Post, July 9, 1990, p. 62.

young Bruce to the great tradition of eastern philosophical thought: Buddha, Confucius, Lao-Tze. Bruce found something he felt passionate about, and became an enthusiastic student for the first time, pouring over books and practicing kung-fu at every opportunity. He missed school regularly, but never missed an after-school session with Yip Man.

Bruce carried this passion for the writings of both martial arts and eastern philosophy into his adult life. After we became friends, I visited him at his home in 1966. He took me to his study and I was amazed, and impressed, at what I saw. The whole room was lined with bookshelves and nearly every book was about martial arts and philosophy.

8

Along with kung fu and philosophy, Bruce began to turn his attention to girls as well—a wonderful way to round out a young man's range of interests, I've always believed! He started to cultivate his appearance, and he learned that his self-confidence and charm could work to his advantage when it came to getting dates. He devoted himself to learning to dance, and in 1958 won the Crown Colony Cha-Cha Championship.

Some of Bruce's fans might find it hard to imagine him cha-cha-ing on the dance floor. Not me. Years ago when I introduced Bruce to my martial arts ballet, he reacted very positively and encouraged me to continue adapting martial arts to dance.

I knew about Bruce's long-held interest in dancing, and therefore, was not surprised when Bruce characterized the ballet I'd created as yet another form of "free expression."

Perhaps I should mention how I came to invent martial arts ballet. In the late 1960s, there was something troubling me—nothing that I had dwelled upon 24 hours a day, seven days a week—but something that was nettlesome nonetheless. I was bothered that I had chosen a profession that deals with so much brutality. How come? I'd ask myself. After all, I am not a violent person, and I'm not happy when I am engaged in violence.

In thinking about this, I wondered what I could create, using my skills, to balance out the inherent violence in taekwondo with something devoid of violence. I considered what makes me happy, and while many things do, most don't lend themselves to martial arts adaptation. But then I thought of dance. I greatly enjoy dancing and listening to music. Everybody loves the greatest of all works of art, which is the human form, and among all things in the universe, we never tire of admiring the contours of the human body. Many of your greatest painters at some point in their lives take on the challenge of painting the female nude.

The engineer—and also the artist in me—had long since appreciated that there is static line beauty and moving line beauty. Even with all of the motion in martial arts, static line and

moving line beauty only stimulate the sense of sight. So I wondered what it would be like to add music to choreographed body
movement, as in Olympic figure skating, ballroom dancing or
gymnastic floor exercise routines. I reasoned that adding music
to choreographed body movement would provide a full stimu-
lating sight-sound experience. That would surely enhance both
the performing/competing experience of the martial artist and
also the spectator experience. I decided to explore this direction.

So I choreographed several dances in ballet-style and set them to
such classical music as Beethoven's Fifth Symphony and the
theme from "Exodus." This creation is the foundation for the
"musical forms" competitions that are now popular at many martial arts tournaments. The art form has found its way to Europe
and Russia. I'm proud to have developed it and thank Bruce for
his initial and steadfast encouragement. Most other martial
artists would have discouraged me and charged me with bas-
tardizing their tradition. But not Bruce. He was always open-
minded to creative projects.

In Hong Kong, after Bruce was expelled from La Salle, he started at the St. Francis Xavier academy, where he became the unof-
ficial boss of the school. He was strong, talked tough, and never
backed down from a fight. One of the brothers convinced Bruce
to represent the school in the boxing ring, whereupon he
knocked out the champion from a nearby school in the first thir-

ty seconds of the first round. I would have loved to have seen that! Can you imagine witnessing Bruce Lee's first organized fight? I expect this victory built Bruce's confidence level, and was a stepping stone to his later success.

But Bruce's time in Hong Kong was drawing to a close. This was a good thing because, even with the benefit of Yip Man's positive influence, Bruce continued to take part in street fights. He even helped arrange illicit contests between students at rival martial arts academies. This sounds like an early and tamer Asian fore-runner of the teenage fist-fighting clubs that have popped up across the United States, beginning in the late-1990s, and that were characterized in the movie "Fight Club," which stars Edward Norton and Brad Pitt. (By the way, for the record, I don't approve of this practice or the culture around it. And I know per-sonally that neither did Bruce Lee as an adult, when he reflected on his teenage years.) These Hong Kong street fights were most-ly friendly sparring matches, but on one occasion, his opponent landed a punch that gave Bruce a black eye. Bruce got mad and unleashed a flurry of strong punches, completely forgetting or unable, in the moment, to gain access to what he had been taught by Yip Man and his study of eastern philosophical thought. Bruce knocked the other boy down, and then kicked his fallen opponent a few times in the eye and the mouth, knocking out a tooth. This attack brought big trouble—and the police.

11

Mrs. Lee had to go down to the police station and sign a document swearing that she would be responsible for Bruce's future behavior. That's when she decided to sit her son down for a serious talk. His mother explained to Bruce that his future in Hong Kong looked bleak at best. He had had a career as a child actor, but that chapter was over. He was a poor student of anything that could be considered a trade or profession. And, he had made some serious enemies among the Hong Kong Mafia, the Triads. Mrs. Lee's solution was bold—and frightening. Bruce should travel to the United States, where he could claim citizenship, and make a fresh start.

In October 1958, at age 18, Bruce set sail for America with $100 in his pocket. He traveled second class, but spent most of the voyage in first class, giving cha-cha lessons. After he arrived in San Francisco, he started out by giving dancing lessons, but found the life of an immigrant with limited English daunting. His mother arranged for a family friend in Seattle, Ruby Chow, to take him in and offer him a job in her restaurant. Bruce and Ruby knocked heads from the very beginning, but she instilled a bit of structure and discipline in his life outside of the martial arts, which he needed as a still adventurous and tempestuous 18-year-old. Over the next two years, Bruce attended Edison Technical School in Seattle and earned a high school diploma. His grades were good enough to gain him entry into the philosophy program at the University of Washington.

At the University of Washington Bruce began to develop his writing skills. Here's an excerpt of an essay he wrote for a freshman English course and published for the first time in Linda's biography of her husband; it recollects his time with Yip Man:

> After four years of hard training in the art of kung fu, I began to understand and felt the principle of gentleness—the art of neutralizing the effect of the opponent's effort and minimizing expenditure of one's energy. All these must be done in calmness and without striving. It sounded simple, but in actual application it was difficult. The moment I engaged in combat with an opponent, my mind was completely perturbed and unstable. Especially after a series of exchanging blows and kicks, all my theory of gentleness was gone. My only one thought left was somehow or another I must beat him and win.

> My instructor Professor Yip Man, head of the Wing Chun School, would come up to me and say, '[Bruce], relax and calm your mind. Forget about yourself and follow your opponent's movement. Let your mind, the basic reality, do the counter-movement without any interfering deliberation. Above all, learn the art of detachment.'

> That was it! I must relax. However, right there I had already done something contradictory, against my will. That was when I said I must relax, the demand for effort in 'must' was already inconsistent with the effortlessness in 'relax.' When my acute self-consciousness grew to what the psychologists called 'double-blind' [sic] type, my instructor would again approach me and say, '[Bruce], preserve yourself by following the natural bend of things and don't interfere. Remember never to assert

13

yourself against nature: never be in frontal opposition to any problem, but control it by swinging with it. Don't practice this week. Go home and think about it.'

The following week I stayed home. After spending many hours in meditation and practice, I gave up and went sailing alone in a junk. On the sea, I thought of all my past training and got mad at myself and punched at the water. Right then at that moment, a thought suddenly struck me. Wasn't this water, the very basic stuff, the essence of kung-fu? I struck it just now, but it did not suffer hurt. Again I stabbed it with all my might, yet it was not wounded. I then tried to grasp a handful of it but it was impossible. This water, the softest substance in the world, could fit into any container. Although it seemed weak, it could penetrate the hardest substance in the world. That was it! I wanted to be like the nature of water.

14

Suddenly a bird flew past and cast its reflection on the water. Right then, as I was absorbing myself, another mystic sense of hidden meaning started upon me. Shouldn't it be the same then that the thoughts and emotions I had in front of an opponent passed like the reflection of the bird over the water? This was exactly what Professor Yip Man meant by being detached—not being without emotion or feeling, but being one in whom feeling was not sticky or blocked. Therefore, in order to control myself I must first accept myself by going with, and not against, my nature. I lay on the boat and felt that I had united with Tao; I had become one with nature. I just lay there and let the boat drift freely and irresistibly according to its own will. For at that moment I had achieved a state of inner feeling in which opposition had become mutually cooperative instead of mutually exclusive, in which there was no longer any conflict in my mind. The whole world to me was unitary[4].

As you see, even as a young man Bruce was a deep thinker. When I first read this, I quietly thanked Yip Man for all he gave my friend, for his ability to get Bruce to reflect and relax. The more I got to know Bruce, the more I realized that he understood himself well and that he knew how to bring serenity into his being. Sometimes, I wish that he would have reflected and found that inner peace more often.

15

---

[4]Lee, p. 37-38.

Chapter Two

My Life as a Boy

"I lived in a cellar for two months...I came out of the cellar on September 28, 1950, ready to fight for my country alongside the Americans."
—Jhoon Rhee

When I consider Bruce's life and look at my own, I see similarities, certainly. But I also see stark differences that intrigue me. I don't think that my early life was better or worse than Bruce's—just vastly different. And, as many people do, I like to examine friendships. What makes friends who are dissimilar in personality and upbringing enjoy each other's company? What makes that friendship click? Let me provide a short biographical chapter on my childhood and young adulthood. I think you'll see our two lives more as a study in contrasts than in similarities.

I was born in a small village, Sanyangri, Asan, Korea, on January 7, 1932—nine years before Bruce's birth. At that time, I was the youngest of three children; and then later, another brother and sister were born. My father was a clerk in a small business, my mother a housewife. The night after I was conceived, my mother had what Koreans call a "taemong," a conception dream. Some years later she told me about this dream. She was in a luxurious palace that was enclosed by a huge castle wall. From outside the castle she heard a tiger roaring at a near-deafening level. The noise woke her up. It was only decades later that I attached meaning to this dream. I think it has to do with the prominence I've been lucky to achieve with my taekwondo activities—the "noise" I've made throughout the world outside my mother's castle: Korea.

18

When I was a baby, a strange thing happened to me. My sister, who was 11 at the time, was babysitting me as she often did. She was a responsible and loving older sibling and was usually very careful with her baby brother. (Note that word "usually.") But one day she was walking around holding me when suddenly, I squirmed and—oops!—slipped out of her grasp and onto a hard floor. The thigh bone between my knee and hip broke. (No, I don't hold a grudge against my sister.) That very same day, my maternal grandfather died. My grieving mother carried me—I was probably crying in pain—five miles to her father's house and, guided by an ancient Korean belief, rubbed her dead father's hand over my broken leg. The fracture healed soon after this unorthodox treatment. (Though I won't say because of it.)

After this traumatic experience, my parents and many other people thought I'd never be very athletic. But I proved them wrong. The fact is, I was always a small child and a slow runner on the playgrounds. I knew early on that I needed to compensate for my small size and lack of foot speed. I decided that I wanted to practice taekwondo. But there were no martial arts studios near my home. So instead, I lifted weights and gained strength.

The main influence on me as a child was my paternal grandfather. He was an upright, stern man with a doctorate in Confucian literature; he offered moral guidance to me in my early years. At one time, when I was five, I lived with my uncle and grandfather for an entire year. My parents sent me there to teach me not to be too dependent, especially on my mother. My grandfather and uncle went to great lengths to teach me respect for my elders, as well as the ways in which a moral person should behave. That is, I was instructed to stand when an elder came into a room and sit only when they gave me permission. I learned to say "sir" or "ma'am" after every sentence I said to an adult. I'd like to think that I have maintained this etiquette, and apparently, some people have noticed. Linda Lee Cadwell once told a friend of mine, "Jhoon Rhee has always been very gentlemanly. He has very high standards of behavior, of how people should behave, and he expects that from other people."

19

My grandfather and uncle also taught me that God is omnipotent and omnipresent. One day my grandfather caught me lying. I had lost a schoolbook and was afraid to tell him so I made up some silly story. I knew it was wrong to lie, and that I deserved the spanking he gave me. He also lectured me. He said, 'My child, don't you know that whenever you lie, cheat or steal, God is watching, and whenever you do a good deed, you are also being watched?' That really stuck with me; I believe it was the most important character-building moment in my life.

My grandfather influenced me in another way: He lived to be 92 years old, in part, because of the series of stretching exercises he would perform every morning. My *RheeShape: Balanced Life Program* of daily mind and body exercises are modeled in part on yoga and the stretches I watched my grandfather do. And, I too expect to live a long life. My goal is to live to 136. I already have plans for my 100th birthday.

After my year with my uncle's family and my grandfather, I went back home. I was overjoyed to be home with my mother and father. But one day, when I was about six years old, I came home from school crying. My mother asked me what was wrong, and I told her how I had been slapped by a tough five-year-old neighbor girl. My mother slapped me hard herself, because she was so disgusted with me for letting myself be assaulted by a girl, and a younger girl at that. I needed to do something to raise my self-confidence, to help me stand on my own two feet. And that's when I started lifting weights, which I continued until I was 13 years old, when I moved to Seoul to enroll at Dong Sung High School. The summer of my 14th year, in 1945, the National Liberation from the Japanese occupation took place. I was too young to understand the full significance of the end of the war, but the idea of freedom from domination would become more significant for me in retrospect, when the North and South of my country went to war in 1950.

All through my schooling, as I've indicated, I had been the smallest child in my class. It was a relief to me when I found a boy in seventh grade who was smaller than me, and we became great friends. But my size made me an easy target for bullies, and I often came home crying. In 1947, when I was fifteen, I enrolled for the first time in a taekwondo academy in Seoul. I didn't dare tell my father for the first three months, because the martial arts had a very poor reputation at that time, and were only slightly better regarded than street fighting. This may strike today's public as odd, considering the respect that martial arts now garner. When my father came to Seoul to visit me, he was upset at my deception, but my uncle persuaded him that he should give me permission to proceed with my training.

The years after World War II seemed to us, at the time, like a complete return to normal life, but with subtle differences—

some cultural. For example, I snuck in to see my first American movies (it was illegal for someone my age to go), and saw the many beautiful American girls come to life for me on the screen. I set a goal for myself then and there that someday I would marry one of those blond American women. Since there were no blond women in Korea, I had no choice but to get to America somehow. But how would I make a living there? How would I support a family? I decided that I would introduce taekwondo to America, and I began to study English with great determination. Over time, my classmates recognized me as the most advanced English student, but very few people knew I studied taekwondo with equal concentration.

Then one day, in the 11th grade, one of the most notorious bullies in my school grabbed a pencil out of my hand. When I politely asked for him to return it, he was rude. I told him I would meet him after school. When we met, I was nervous (I was only a brown belt then), but I quickly went on the offensive, giving him a black eye and a kick in the throat. He capitulated. When the other students saw him the next day, they asked questions, and his answers raised my status at the school. I received much more respect after that, and felt strong and confident at school.
I graduated from high school in 1950, and was accepted to Dong Kook University. I had barely gotten settled there, when the Korean War broke out on June 25, 1950. At first, my nine-year-old brother and I fled south, to be with my grandfather, but then we

decided to go back to our home in Suwon, because my mother was there all alone. We traveled the 50 miles on foot, over three days. We were attacked from the air many times, and relied on friendly strangers taking us in and feeding us as we made our way back to our mother. We finally found her. Thankfully reunited with her, we were overcome with tears and prayers.

We stayed with her there, but by August I had to begin a new life underground. I was 18 years old, and if I had been seen by the neighbors, I would have been forced to register, and sooner or later, I would have been drafted into the North Korean army. I lived in a cellar for two months, until after the Americans had landed and pushed the Communist army north beyond Pyongyang. I came out of the cellar on September 28, 1950, ready to fight for my country alongside the Americans. In November, I joined a unit of the U.S. Air Force as an interpreter. Over the course of the next year, I worked as an interpreter for the Americans and the British, and then was drafted into the South Korean army. Life was so bad in my unit, the 101st Battalion, that I applied to officer cadet training school. Casualties in the cadet officer corps were over 70 percent, but anything was better than the hunger and cold in my battalion, which was caused by my commanding officer's corruption. You see, at our expense, he would keep most of our food and supplies for himself and his friends or sell it on the black market.

So, I prepared myself to die, and I'm not being melodramatic because that is a fact. I wrote my parents telling them that the officers at my cadet training program had decided to keep me on as a taekwondo instructor, so that no one would worry about me. (I wonder if my dad was thankful that my uncle had persuaded him to allow me to study martial arts?) And then, when the situation seemed hopeless, the truce was declared, on July 27, 1953. All of the 250 cadets in my class felt we had been reprieved from certain death. I was overjoyed; and now I could pursue my dream of teaching taekwondo in the United States.

After my graduation as an officer, I applied for army aviation training, but I soon changed over to weather and aircraft maintenance. When I completed my training, I was assigned to train others. I taught weather and maintenance for a year and a half. At that time, I heard about an opportunity to train in aircraft maintenance in the United States. I felt that this was my chance, and I was determined to make the most of it. I applied, along with 50 others, and was one of only three chosen to go. My proficiency in English was the deciding factor. I landed in San Francisco in early June of 1956.

Chapter Three

Bruce Gains a Measure of Fame

"He had something the others didn't have —you could see it in the way he explained his art, in the way he talked. He was utterly dynamic that night and one couldn't help being drawn to him. Even those who knew very little about the arts found themselves listening to him intently [5]."

A few years after I arrived in the United States, Bruce—in a different West Coast city, for different reasons—had decided to teach in a formal setting, as well. Here is where our lives are similar, although the form of martial arts we taught was very different. In 1962, he launched a kwoon, a martial arts academy, in Seattle. He had attracted informal sparring partners and proteges since he had started giving informal lessons, in San Francisco, but now he felt ready to offer a full course of training in the art he was developing, "jeet kune do." "Jeet kune do" translates as "the way of the intercepting fist," and is based on Bruce's realization of "the way that is no way." Bruce was careful not to

[5]Observer of Bruce Lee at Ed Parker's First International Karate Championships, 1964, from Lee p. 70.

refer to jeet kune do as a method or school of martial arts, since he had strong opinions about traditional methods of teaching martial arts. He made many enemies in the traditional schools by calling their rituals and stances "baloney," and asking what was the use of breaking boards and performing stylized moves when street fighting was a fluid, ever-changing set of circumstances. That's Bruce—the rebel. Although, as you'll see later, he eventually changed his mind about the merits of board-breaking.

His kwoon had only been open for a short time when Linda Emery walked in. Bruce had come to Linda's high school to talk about Asian philosophy, and she had been taken with him right away. She was a 17-year-old high school senior at the time. Bruce was a 22-year-old sophomore in college. A few months later, after Linda casually expressed an interest in Bruce, she was challenged by one of her classmates to investigate kung-fu. She was apprehensive at first, but decided to see what this man and his school were all about. She was taken enough with the world of kung-fu, and the dashing young man, that she began to take regular lessons. They were a perfect match, as I would find out later when I got to know them both.

Before that happened, Bruce had decided to leave college, at the end of his junior year. His kwoon was doing well enough by then that he felt he could leave it in the charge of his lieutenant, Taky Kimura, and start a second one in California with another kung-fu teacher,

James Lee (not related to Bruce). At this point, Bruce's ambition was to start a chain of kung-fu schools across the country, and opening a second school in Oakland would be a crucial test of his plans. Although Linda and Bruce were deeply involved with each other, she still hadn't told her parents that she was dating a Chinese man, and he was reluctant to commit to her without the means to support a family. Therefore, he moved down to Oakland alone, to pave the way. During the summer of 1964, Bruce and Linda exchanged letters, and after two and half months, Bruce asked her to marry him. She very happily agreed.

They decided that the best course of action was to elope. In Seattle at that time, in order to obtain a marriage license, one had to fill out the necessary papers, and then wait for three days. But prospective newlyweds automatically had their names published on the "Vital Statistics" page of the newspaper. An aunt of Linda's saw that Linda C. Emery and J. F. Lee were to be married, and a family council of war was inevitable. There were recriminations, hurt feelings, reasoned arguments and emotional outbursts, but in the end, no one was able to talk the young couple out of their plan. Eventually, Linda's mother came to love Bruce as one of the family, but it was an inauspicious beginning. The newlyweds made their farewells, and moved to James Lee's house in Oakland.

Later in 1964, Bruce tasted his first real bite of fame, and success came about in an unlikely way. Ever since he and Linda moved

27

back to California, Bruce had been taking part in many martial arts tournaments and exhibitions. He was invited by our mutual friend Ed Parker to his karate tournament, the First International Karate Championships, held in Long Beach in 1964, which, as I mentioned earlier, is where I met Bruce. Not many people knew about kung-fu at that time, and Ed wanted Bruce to demonstrate his technique for the large crowd of West Coast black belts and instructors who would be present. Ed decided to film his demonstration, which would turn out to be very important to Bruce's career.

In the audience that night, along with all the instructors, were many amateurs and fans of the martial arts, including a Beverly Hills hair stylist named Jay Sebring. Jay later became Bruce's good friend, and, in fact, was the man who brought him together with Steve McQueen. Tragically, Jay was one of the people killed by Charles Manson in the director Roman Polanski's house the night Manson's "family" murdered the actress Sharon Tate and her guests. But in 1964, Jay Sebring's presence in the audience at the championships was fortuitous for Bruce.

Like me, Jay was very impressed with Bruce's demonstration, and found out that Ed Parker had filmed it. It seems the demo stuck in Jay's mind, because a few days later, when he was cutting William Dozier's hair, Bruce's name came back to Jay. Dozier was a television producer, whose credits included "Gunsmoke," "Perry Mason," and the television series "Batman," which was

28

then in production. He mentioned to Jay that he was looking for a good-looking, young Chinese man to play Charlie Chan's son in a new series. Jay told Dozier about his impression of Bruce at Ed Parker's tournament—that he had charisma and a good sense of humor, and that he was very good at the martial arts.

Bruce's Funny Streak

Indeed, Bruce did have a good sense of humor. He cracked jokes very spontaneously. Let me jump ahead a few years from this story about Bruce's career to share some real-life examples of how he could get you laughing. In 1967, I went to a martial arts convention sponsored by *Black Belt* magazine where I was to give a speech. Bruce was there, and we were sitting on a bench outside the convention hall, waiting for a speaker to reach the podium and address the audience. When Bruce saw who the speaker was, he rolled his eyes, sighed and whispered to me, "Last summer, this guy talked so much he got sunburned under his tongue."

Here's another one Bruce told me, which I subsequently told Larry King on a radio show: "A Japanese emperor wanted to hire a great martial arts bodyguard. There were several candidates, among them a Japanese samurai, who went to the emperor to audition. The emperor asked, "What can you do?' So the samurai opened up a matchbox and a fly flew out of it. The samurai whipped out his sword and cut the fly in half. A second

Japanese samurai came and did the same thing, except he went one better. He cut the fly into four pieces. Then a Jewish samurai came with his assistant. Very dramatically, he asked his assistant to open the box. The fly flew out and the Jewish samurai swung his sword at it. But the fly kept flying. The emperor said, 'Too bad. You missed.' The Jewish samurai said, 'Ahh, but Your Majesty, I think upon closer examination you'll see the fly has been circumcised.'"

As Linda once told me, " I remember thinking when I was going out with Bruce that I was just laughing all the time. He was so much fun. He had a phenomenal way of, first, remembering jokes and then of telling them. And he was always amusing people on the set with his magic tricks."

30

Bruce also had fun with the press. In 1967, at a press conference during his Kato fame, he joked to reporters in a self-deprecating way. "I possess the yellow belt," he said. "It signifies that I can run pretty damn fast." Later during a luncheon with the media, he poked fun at his Chinese ancestry. He was served soup and joked, "Now how in hell am I supposed to eat this with chopsticks?[6]"

The Call Comes In

But Bruce's real magic was his martial arts and magnetic personality. So, back in Los Angeles, Bill Dozier decided to try to capi-

---

[6]William Clopton, Jr., "Kato Likes Puns, Preys on Words," *The Washington Post*, May 6, 1967, P. B3.

talize on Bruce's talents and dynamics. But first he had to be convinced of Bruce's potential. He asked Jay to get in touch with Ed Parker, so that he could see the film Parker had shot of Bruce. Parker agreed to come out to Twentieth Century Fox Studios, where he screened the film. Dozier was impressed, and called Bruce in Oakland. He was out, and Linda took the call; she couldn't get him to tell her why he was calling, but the couple had a very hopeful feeling from the call. When Bruce returned Dozier's call, he asked him if he would be interested in testing for the part of Number-One Son in a new TV series to be called, appropriately enough, "Number-One Son." Bruce agreed. He flew to L.A. and auditioned, and then returned to Oakland to wait and hear what the powers-that-be thought of his performance.

31

In the meantime, Linda gave birth to the couple's first child, Brandon, in February 1965. Daughter Shannon would be born in 1969. I saw both Shannon and Brandon quite a bit when they were kids and loved them very much. But shortly after Brandon's birth, word came that Bruce's father had died in Hong Kong. Bruce felt immensely sad over his father's death, but also joy that his father knew about the birth of his first grandson before he died. Bruce naturally flew over to pay his respects. He had a special penance to do because he had been away when his father died. The ancient custom says that when a son returns after his father has died, he must "come crawling back" to either the funeral or the grave.

When he arrived at the mortuary where his father lay before being buried, Bruce crawled from the door to the casket, wailing. I remember when Bruce told me this story a few years later. I could see by his facial expressions that this was such a very difficult trip for him. He felt so many emotions: deep sadness, of course; guilt, as part of the natural human condition for moments of intimacy not realized between a father and a son; anxiety, over the uncertain twists and turns his career was taking; and I believe remorse, because his father could not experience what Bruce foresaw as his impending success in the United States.

When he got back to Oakland, Bruce found out that the TV series was to be put on hold, and soon heard that it would be cancelled. But Bill Dozier had another idea. He wanted to wait and see what the public reaction to "Batman" would be. If people liked one cartoon-based series, Dozier thought the next step should be another comic strip on TV: "The Green Hornet." This changed the whole picture for Bruce and Linda. Dozier put my friend under option to play the part of Kato, who was, of course, the Green Hornet's right-hand man. But it would be a year before Bruce found out whether "The Green Hornet" would go into production.

Linda and Bruce decided to take the option money and go for an extended visit to Hong Kong, so his family could get to know Linda. The couple moved into the house on Nathan Road, where Bruce grew up. There was some friction, however, because Bruce's son Brandon was very young and his mother and sister were convinced that Linda didn't know how to raise the boy. What's more, Linda spoke almost no Cantonese. The family of three lived in that house for four months, hearing now and then from Dozier, always positive things, but never what they wanted to hear, that the show was a go. Linda and her in-laws gradually got to know each other, and of course, Brandon was very well cared for.

Bruce told me once that during this time, he'd often venture deep into introspection about his life and career. He settled the details of his father's estate, and spent a lot of time in self-criticism and self-analysis, wondering how he would provide for his family. He never considered going back to the film industry in Hong Kong, even though he had made so many films as a child star and could probably parlay that experience into some starring roles as an adult. He made no effort to contact his old friends in the studios, although he took Brandon to meet his old teacher Yip Man, and had a picture taken of the two of them together. (Again, this shows the sort of deep affinity that Bruce held for his instructor.) Bruce wanted to make it big in America, and he knew if he could just hang on long enough, his art would bring him what he wanted and needed.

Linda, Brandon and Bruce returned to the United States in September of 1965, to stay with Linda's family in Seattle. It was difficult waiting without knowing what would come next, although

33

Linda's family did start to get to know and accept Bruce. Eventually, Bruce and Linda decided to move back down to Oakland.

They had barely moved, when word came from Bill Dozier that "The Green Hornet" was indeed a go. Shooting would start in June. I would have loved to have seen Bruce's face when he got word. When he was happy, he didn't hide it, and on that day he was ecstatic, I'm sure. The Lees packed up again and moved to Los Angeles in March of 1966, to a very small apartment in Westwood. It was the first time Linda and Bruce had a place of their own. Twentieth Century Fox set up Bruce with a few lessons from an acting coach named Jeff Cory, which ended up being the only formal acting training he ever received.

Chapter Four

My Life in the States:
From Engineer to Entrepreneur

"Bruce Lee...convinced me that blindly following tradition leads to stagnation in the martial arts."
—Jhoon Rhee

Unlike Bruce, I came to the United States of my own accord, and I always remember my first impressions of this country. When I arrived here in 1956, I was unprepared for the splendor of America—the cars, the skyscrapers, the wealth—that was so prevalent during those prosperous post-war years. I was taken with the many neon signs and the beautiful American women, just like the ones I had seen in the films. I was only in San Francisco for a day, then I flew to Austin, Texas, and then traveled by bus to Gary Air Force Base, in San Marcos, Texas. I found the routine of the base very familiar because of my own military experience, and although I was the only Asian for miles around, I was treated with respect as an officer in a foreign army. But I longed to make friends, and to see if I had any chance to fulfill my dream and somehow stay in America. I joined the local Methodist church, where I was welcomed and made to feel comfortable. Over the coming months, I let my new friends from the church know of my wish to stay and study in America, and they began to work together to try to help me. I needed a sponsor who would vouch for my character and promise to support me if necessary.

As my time in the training program ran out, I began to lose hope, because my friends and I couldn't find a sponsor. It got down to the last Sunday. I attended church as usual, and the pastor asked the congregation if anyone could find it in his or her heart to come forward to help me. To my surprise and delight, an elderly man and his wife spoke up. His name was Robert L. Bunting, a local real estate broker who wanted to help me further my education; I was overcome with relief and joy, and later on he and his wife became my foster parents.

I had to go back to Korea for one more year to finish out my term of enlistment, but as soon as I received my honorable discharge and completed the paperwork, I returned to the United States as a student, in November of 1957. I enrolled at the San Marcos Southwest State College in February of 1958, and I began my studies. In the middle of 1960, I transferred to the University of Texas in Austin to study engineering. I intended to finish my degree there in three years, but my life took a different turn in the summer of 1962.

I accepted an offer of a job in a karate school in Washington, D.C. But when I arrived there, I found that there were only six students! The enrollment was so low, the school couldn't even afford to pay me to teach. I then decided to open my own school, and fortunately it was a great success. Within twelve weeks, I had more than 100 students and was able to make a good living. My American dream was starting to come true. I never did go back to the University of Texas, to complete my engineering degree, but instead embarked on an intensive path of constant self-learning from all the people and books and experiences around me. Since then, I have been awarded an honorary degree. Today, there are Jhoon Rhee Studios around the United States (and many more around the world), with eight in the Washington area. I have had the privilege of teaching many famous students, including senators, congressmen, diplomats, royalty and athletes.

Congressional Speech

I would like to share with readers more about my life and what the American freedom system established by our Founding Fathers has allowed me to achieve. Rather than interrupt the flow of this narrative, I have instead included in the appendix a speech that was delivered April 11, 2000 on the floor of the U.S. House of Representatives by Michigan Rep. Nick Smith. Nick Smith is a friend of mine, and as you will read, was inspired when I was recognized as one of the top 200 immigrants in American history.

Although my teaching has been highly successful, at times, like my friend Bruce Lee, I have generated a little controversy—mainly because I do not teach the traditional taekwondo forms I learned in Korea. I have continually adapted and modified my approach to martial arts as I have refined my own ideas and skills and had a chance to observe others. I owe a great debt to Bruce Lee for this approach. Bruce was an inspiration to me while he was alive and, perhaps even more so when I reflect on all he did for me. He convinced me that blindly following tradition leads to stagnation in the martial arts. Whereas I respect the traditional approach, I do not believe there is any one "best" style—not mine, not anyone else's. The most important thing to me has always been to bring the benefits of martial arts and fitness to as many people as possible. There are many paths.

Bruce's teaching, his movies above all, helped to create the booming interest in the martial arts around the world in the 1970s. I have followed my own path in developing the Jhoon Rhee style of taekwondo in America, while honoring other approaches in taekwondo, and the many other positive martial arts disciplines, such as judo, kung-fu, tai chi, aikido, karate, fencing and others.

Chapter Five

Befriending Each Other

"...he casually walked behind me and grabbed me from behind as if he were attacking me. In self-defense, I stomped on his instep, gave him a wicked elbow and threw him over my shoulder to the floor."
—Linda Lee Cadwell

Although "The Green Hornet" only had a six-month run on the air (during the 1966-7 season), it launched Bruce's career as an action movie star. The show got mixed reviews, but his performance as Kato generated bags of fan mail, and earned the show cult status. Off camera, Bruce obviously enjoyed his taste of fame. He found time to ride on parade floats, put in appearances at supermarket openings and attend autograph-signings, always dressed in his black Kato costume. And, as I said earlier, he also attended my tournaments. Bruce taped TV and radio spots, which, as I've explained, is how the two of us got reconnected in 1966. As he traveled around the country, he also gave many newspaper interviews. It became obvious that he was more than a body builder with fast reflexes. One interviewer wrote: "When he isn't playing the cold-eyed Kato, Lee is the complete ham, alternately the pixie and the tough kid on the block. He puns unmercifully, performs dazzling feats of speed and coordination, wades bravely into the riptides of a language he is trying to master. [Here are two examples] of Bruce's wit: 'Seven hundred million Chinese cannot be Wong,' or 'I don't drink or smoke. But I do chew gum, because Fu Man Chu.'[7]"

As I've mentioned, it was during these years that Bruce and I became close friends, so I know how much he relished becoming famous. He'd always get a twinkle in his eye when he talked about his growing following of fans. But he'd never gloat to me about his fame, and he never let it get to his head the way it does to so many celebrities. Furthermore, although he'd tease me and play jokes on me—that was his playful nature—he'd always treat me with the highest regard, and, of course, I always admired him, too.

Now about his spirited and fun-loving personality. Earlier I had mentioned a stunt he orchestrated at one of my tournaments—I think it was the 1970 championships. Here's how Linda recently recalled it to me:

> A couple of times I went with Bruce to your tournaments. And, as you remember, those were golden times for

40

karate tournaments, in the mid-60s, because it was some-thing new to the American public. And, you were very successful and highly respected even then in Washington, D.C. There was an electricity in the air back then about karate tournaments. I remember what great turnouts you had. Bruce added even more excitement to the atmosphere. It was great. At one of your events, Bruce and I had a part together. We had planned a stunt that we wanted to pull. I was there and my son Brandon was too, although he was just a baby.

I was wearing a fancy new dress. I loved that dress so much, partly because in those days, despite Bruce's emerg-ing fame, we had trouble rubbing dimes together, as they say. So I didn't buy many new clothes. The dress was very colorful; it had yellow, blue, green and red diagonal stripes, and it was sleeveless. I was also wearing heels. Now the point is, I didn't look like I was dressed to do what we had planned to do. Bruce was doing his demonstration for all of your participants and crowd members, and suddenly he stopped and invited me up on the stage. I came up on the stage and he introduced me to the audience. As he was doing this, he casually walked behind me and grabbed me from behind as if he were attacking me. In self-defense, I stomped on his instep, gave him a wicked elbow and threw him over my shoulder to the floor. It was so totally unex-pected, the audience was speechless for a moment. Then they realized it was all a gag and they laughed and laughed. It was really fun. Bruce had thought up the stunt and we had practiced it enough to make it work.

41

I remember that gag very well, and Linda tells the story just as it happened. The crowd erupted in a combination of laughter and

42

wild applause. I was taken completely by surprise and remember Bruce looking over at me, after he picked himself up off the floor and pretended to gather his bearings. He flashed me a devilish smile. He could see that I got such a kick out of the antics. I was also impressed with Linda's role. She's strong and agile! Although most of the people who were then practicing martial arts and were on hand that day were boys and men, I bet the few girls and young women watching gained some inspiration from Linda. I know the stunt caused quite a buzz at the demos that year. And, I also know that Linda helped to stir more female interest in martial arts.

You know what a good feeling it is when you hear that someone you love and admire also thinks very well of you? Well, I had this experience with Linda. She is an extremely gracious person who goes out of her way to be supportive of others. She recently told one of my acquaintances about the quality of the friendship Bruce and I developed and what he thought of me. "Bruce had great respect for Jhoon Rhee's martial arts and the way he ran his schools," she said. "He always considered Jhoon quite a groundbreaker in putting on these highly regarded tournaments. They shared a goal of wanting to expose the American public to real martial arts—more than just the kicking and punching—the discipline and the underlying philosophy. I remember Bruce saying this about Jhoon: 'He is a serious martial artist. Not just a fly-by-nighter, not just someone who got his black belt in ten easy lessons or something.'"

Bruce was respectful of all his friends and, as I've suggested, he was picky about who he chose to socialize with. "Bruce was very selective in choosing friends," Linda told me. "He didn't want to spend a lot of time with a bunch of business acquaintances. He'd rather have a few good friends. He valued his time greatly, and he spent a lot of his time reading and, of course, performing his craft. He didn't go to many large parties, because he didn't want to be a glad-hander. He wanted one-on-one relationships. And to this day those buddies of Bruce are still good friends. We started the Bruce Lee Educational Foundation and these are the guys who are doing much of the work."

Linda is referring to such former students of Bruce as Taky Kimura, Ted Wong, Richard Bustillo, Bob Bremer, Herb Jackson, Pete Jacobs, Allen Joe, George Lee, Daniel Lee, Gregion Lee, Steve Golden, and Jerry Poteet. They were joined by second generation students Andrew Kimura, Tommy Gong, Chris Kent, Cass Magda, Tim Tackett and John Little on the board of the Foundation. Of course, Linda and her daughter Shannon are also on the Board.

In addition, martial arts stars Mike Stone, Chuck Norris and Joe Lewis—who for years were the best fighters in the country—all trained with Bruce. I remember Bruce called me one time and, during our conversation, told me how proud he was about the quality of people who chose him to be their teacher.

Joe Lewis: From Dubious Critic to Devoted Student

I remember the occasion well when I first met one of those students, Joe Lewis, in 1966. He was the first person to show up for my tournament in that year. He came to watch but, thanks to a little prodding, ended up competing and winning just about everything. Here's how Joe described the story to a colleague of mine: "When I was still in the Marine Corps, in 1966, we were very anti-tournament competition. We thought other schools didn't train very hard, and most did not, in fact. So we didn't want to have anything to do with karate tournaments. But in May 1966, I decided to check out Jhoon Rhee's National Championships. So I went north to D.C. from my [U.S. Marine Corps] camp in North Carolina to see the tournament. Being a good little marine, I got there early and was the only person there. Two Korean gentlemen—one was Jhoon—were in their office. They asked who I was and invited me into their office. I was very humble. When they found out I was a black belt, they asked me to compete. I didn't want to, but finally they convinced me to fill out an application and compete the next morning.

"The next day I arrived early again, got my gi on and got all warmed up. I had to wait a long time—from 9:00 to 5:00, and that's the last time I showed up on time for a competition—but I won first place in the black belt competition. I won the grand championship and I won first place in kata [the dancing form of

44

martial arts]. I had only one point scored against me the whole day in my very first tournament. People say it was like an amateur golfer going straight to the U.S. Open and winning on his first try. So Jhoon Rhee, who I respect a lot, was the man who started my fighting career by talking me into the competition. I think that's very significant."

Believe me, I was glad I was able to convince Joe to compete. His performances during that tournament were simply incredible. He went on to become one of the most talented and well-known martial artists in the world. And in a 1990s magazine poll of prominent champions, Joe was named by his peers "the greatest karate fighter of all time."

45

Joe credits Bruce with helping him unlock new ways of competing in martial arts, new ways of thinking about this wonderful craft. But his introduction into the world of Bruce Lee had inauspicious beginnings. Joe recently told me the story of how he met Bruce and his first impressions of this legend. "I first met Bruce Lee at [Washington, D.C.'s] Mayflower Hotel in 1967, where I was staying during your tournament. He was a guest and I was the defending champion from the United States National Karate Championships. I was on the cover of the brochure for your tournament along with Bruce [and another martial artist]. I had never heard of Bruce Lee. I wasn't fond of kung-fu guys or Chinese stylists. They weren't much into the fighting part of it. He introduced himself, and I said hello."

Joe ran into Bruce again several months later at the offices of *Black Belt* magazine, where, as I've suggested, Bruce spent a lot of time. Once again, Joe was not impressed. "As I was going to my car this little kung-fu guy comes running outside," Joe told me. "He said, 'Joe Lewis, can I talk to you?' He reintroduced himself and started talking about his style of martial arts and why it was different from what existed at that time. It was all going in one ear and out the other, though. Here I am facing a kung-fu guy, a little guy, a Chinese guy. I was very prejudiced at that time against non-fighting styles and little people, period. I was a big weight lifter and wasn't impressed by people who didn't look athletic."

But Joe started talking to his friend Mike Stone, who was one of Bruce's students and a dynamic martial artist in his own right. "The more Mike talked about the instruction he was getting from Bruce, the more he appealed to my fighter side," Joe said. "He was talking about such concepts as out-thinking your opponent, working on the trigger squeeze [the explosion at the moment of attack], being able to cue your trigger squeeze in a deceptive way, and using your lead hand and lead leg as opposed to rear hand and leg as the superior weapons. So that caught my attention. Mike and I talked again and he convinced me that I should give Bruce Lee another chance, look him up and have him teach me what he was teaching Mike."

Bruce did, and soon Joe and he became good friends. Joe recalls all the help that Bruce extended to him and how he was so proud that someone of Bruce's caliber was taking such a devoted interest in his career: "Bruce would come to the tournaments when I'd fight. I'd bring him on stage and introduce him as my instructor. He would give me support and advice and even give me a little quote to say into the microphone every time I'd win." Joe says giving Bruce Lee "another chance" was one of the best decisions he ever made as a martial artist.

Reviewers Praise Bruce

Writers often heaped mountains of praise on Bruce, in many of the newspaper articles about him in 1967. One reviewer wrote, "Those who watched him would bet on Bruce to render Cassius Clay senseless if they were put in a room and told that anything goes[8]." Now, Bruce was a great admirer of Cassius Clay, who of course changed his name to Muhammad Ali. Ali likewise told me years later that he admired Bruce, as well. Later, I'll relate the story of my relationship with "The Greatest" and how I was able to connect the two of them, even though they never met!

47

Another reviewer said that Bruce "...strikes with such speed that he makes a rattler look like a study in slow motion[9]." Although I'm still fond of my electron metaphor for Bruce's quickness, I like that one too. Or how about this one, which I think I once told

[8]Lee, p. 74.
[9]Ibid.

Bruce: "Bruce Lee is so fast he can turn off the light switch and be in bed and under the covers before the room gets dark." It's amazing to think about it—but Bruce was so fast that his moves couldn't be captured on film! He had once told me he had to force himself to slow down his technique so that it could be captured by the cameras. At his normal lightning-fast speed the cameras only could catch a blurry image of flying fists and feet.

There was another side to Bruce's new-found popularity, though. As the number of his fans grew, their need to get close to him became overwhelming, and sometimes dangerous. He once told an interviewer for *Black Belt* magazine: "It can be a terrifying experience sometimes. After a personal appearance at Madison Square Garden at a karate tournament, I started to make an exit, escorted by three karate men. I was practically mobbed as I approached the main lobby, and I had to make a hasty exit through a side door. In Fresno, California, I was scratched, kicked and gouged by riotous fans. I just couldn't protect myself without doing bodily harm to my fans, whose aim, after all, was not to hurt me[10]."

48

I don't think I ever talked to Bruce about that particular hasty and hectic exit, but I'm sure he did the best he could not to hurt anyone. Still, he had to be on guard because sometimes your enemies pretend to be your fans and try to hurt you.

---

[10]Lee, p. 80.

He was cautious about that. He probably would still be dealing with some of those mob scenes and, if he were alive today and came to me for advice on the subject, I'd tell him about my slogan: "Nothing bothers me." For years in the Washington, D.C. area, I ran ads for my schools that read: "Nobody Bothers Me." Then, to my delight, my son started saying at age three, "Nobody bothers me, either." Eventually, the phrase changed into "Nothing bothers me." So, I would tell Bruce not to worry, to take a deep breath and smile your way through a mob. If things are beyond your control, you just face it and go through with it. I know I always try to deal with fans very cordially. I really enjoy them, as did Bruce most of the time. I treat every individual as equal to me. That's just the way I am. We really are created equally, as Thomas Jefferson made so clear in the Declaration of Independence.

49

Anyway, after "The Green Hornet" went off the air, Bruce's show business career slowed down for almost two years. He made cameo appearances on network television: "Blondie," "Ironside," and "Here Come the Brides." For several months, he helped the producer Fred Weintraub develop the pilot for the Warner Brothers TV series "Kung Fu," with the understanding that Bruce would play the lead character. It seemed like the right part at the right time: a series about a Chinese martial arts master in America, trying to discover truths about himself and his adopted country. But Bruce didn't get the role; he was devastated when NBC and its sponsors decided to cast David Carradine instead. The movers-and-shakers believed America wasn't ready to watch a Chinese actor play the lead in a prime time network series. Bruce got the disappointing news by telegram, in Hong Kong. As much as I like David Carradine for his acting, I think Bruce would have been much better playing "Grasshopper," as the character was sometimes called. To earn a living between television jobs, Bruce went back to teaching jeet kune do. Now that he had a certain amount of celebrity, he was able to raise his rates, and to charge even higher prices for a small group of Hollywood proteges, who included the actors Chuck Norris, Steve McQueen, James Coburn, James Garner, and Lee Marvin, the basketball star Kareem Abdul-Jabbar, the director Roman Polanski, and the writer/producer Stirling Silliphant, all of whom became Bruce's devoted friends.

50

James Coburn had learned some karate for his role in "Our Man Flint," but he found Bruce's technique completely different. He told Linda the following for her book about Bruce's life, which I include here because I think Coburn's words demonstrate Bruce's unique ability to connect with his students, teaching them to open their minds, center their bodies and direct their spirits:

"His method of teaching was not teaching at all in the accepted sense—it was evolving through certain ideas, teaching you tools, finding out your strong points, your weak points...He always had this energy. It was always exploding on him, though he channeled it whenever possible, which was most of the time. I mean he actually created this energy within himself. He always got more force from doing something, for instance. We'd work out together for an hour and a half and at the end of that time he'd be filled with force. You felt really high when you finished working out with Bruce[11]."

51

[11]Lee, p. 75.

Chapter Six

The Letters Begin

*" [Bruce] loved reading about
a wide diversity of martial arts
and philosophy subjects...my friend
studied philosophy in college
and was one of the greatest
martial arts philosophers. "*
—*Jhoon Rhee*

Bruce first started writing letters to me in the spring of 1968
(see a copy of the letter on page 56). Receiving a letter from
Bruce, I must tell you, was an event. When I'd leaf through
my daily mail—with all of its bills and publications and
junk mail—I'd always stop and smile when I saw a return
address from Bruce Lee. I knew I was in for a treat because
he wrote with passion and conviction, and with substance
and style. Bruce wrote, in fact, just as he spoke—with
charismatic articulation.

Of course, in those days, we didn't have the fantastic communication devices that are standard in today's fast-lane, high-tech

54

world. We didn't have the instant gratification of a computer, a fax machine, a modem, or even the common telephone answering machine. Most business people, myself included, used a typewriter to compose letters to our friends and associates. Bruce usually wrote his letters in longhand. A handwritten letter is extremely personal. Sheer penmanship alone—and Bruce's was very artistic—reveals a lot about the writer. (For more on this, see the section I've included in this book from Koshu Morioka, one of the world's leading handwriting analysts, which, I think, offers another glimpse inside the world of Bruce Lee.)

What's more, it often takes more time to compose a handwritten letter, because you can't correct your mistakes, as you can on a typewriter, when putting pen to paper. So your thoughts and words have to flow naturally. A few years after this first letter, I gave Bruce a gift to show my appreciation for all he'd done for me; it was an IBM executive typewriter, the best on the market at that time. You'll see later on that he does begin to type some of his correspondence. The letters were also extra-special to me because I knew that Bruce's time was stretched so thin. He always kept a very busy schedule filled with professional commitments, martial arts training, reading and, of course, the demands of a family life.

Letter One

In this first letter, which really doesn't demonstrate as much passion and substance as do subsequent letters, you'll see Bruce's mention of pictures for my program. He was talking about the program for the Jhoon Rhee National Championships. From 1968 to 1970, Bruce would mail me copies of all the advertising used by Los Angeles-area martial arts studios to help my own advertising campaign in Washington, D.C. These included the ads used by the Chuck Norris Studio, Ed Parker's Studios and other reputable schools. You can tell that, while Bruce was generous to provide me with this precious material, he was also attentive to detail. Note that he directs me to use all four pictures on one page. He even said that twice. I didn't mind his guidance on this matter as he had a keen sense of presentation, even in graphic design! Furthermore, the care he shows here was intended to benefit me and my tournament.

When Bruce came that year to my tournament, he performed many of the moves that I'd seen before. But he still impressed me, and for those who had never seen Bruce perform, I'm sure the demo was awe-inspiring. He'd do two-finger pushups at my demos, and one-inch punches to knock down a 250-pound man. He'd block punches blindfolded with an opponent jabbing away at close contact. The most impressive thing was his quickness but also his sheer strength. Here is a man who weighed not much more than 150 pounds and yet he was capable of generating 150-

Letter One

Jhoon,

Enclosed are the pictures and negatives for your program. I have carefully select[ed] those that will be most appropriate; I wish you will arrange them and put all of them in—that is, four on the one page and the small portrait on the instructor's page.

First of all, I hope you will take very good care of the two negatives because I need them. This is important—do give your attention to this matter.

Under the small portrait (the one for the referees & jury, or the instructor's page), the wording should be: BRUCE LEE, PRESIDENT – JEET KUNE DO.

Including the two negatives, there will be four pictures for the one full page. The two negatives are action pictures. Then one picture (the half long one) is by myself, the other one is with my Kato uniform with Van, the Green Hornet. Arrange them the way you see fit, but do include all four of them in that page.

Of course, as soon as the program is out send one to me.

Take Care
Bruce

P.S. take good care of the negatives
TOTAL: -- 3 PICTURES + 2 NEGATIVES

mile-per-hour, hurricane-force winds, so to speak. The crowds were exhilarated by his speed and power. But as Linda and I have discussed, Bruce didn't often perform these maneuvers; he felt they did not demonstrate true martial arts. But he did for me at my venue because he knew they were sensational and would captivate the audience. He would always do them as part of a larger and more comprehensive demo that did include moves in the "true" martial arts spirit.

Letter Two

Bruce's second letter to me came in early June 1968, as my annual tournament was drawing nearer; it was scheduled to open on June 23. I was looking forward to seeing Bruce when he arrived for my tournament and anticipated spending hours with him at my house—eating, talking, eating, kicking-and-punching and eating some more. For a couple of relatively small Asian-Americans we sure could put away food. Thank goodness my wife was a good cook!

I had recently told Bruce that Chuck Norris and Mike Stone had agreed to come and perform demos at the championships, and Bruce writes that their inclusion will "nicely" round-out the exhibition schedule. Bruce's happiness that he'd be joined at the event by two other star martial artists shows the sincere good-spirited fraternity of the martial arts community. It also indicates that Bruce had confidence that Chuck and Mike would not, in any way, steal any of his thunder; no one could upstage Mr. Lee, even if they wanted to (which they probably didn't anyway). Joe Lewis could not make it and Bruce was simply assuring me that even without Joe, all would be just fine. Bruce was confident that the tournament would be a big success, as it always had been since its inception in 1964.

I must have recently acknowledged to him some concern I had about the Poor People's March on Washington, planned to coincide with the championships. Some 50,000 people were expected to rally on the Mall—and at least that many came. If I remember correctly, I was a tad worried that people who wanted to come to the tournament might not go because of traffic tie-ups caused by the marchers, or worse, fear for their personal safety. Initially, the protesters listened to the organizers' requests, including those from the honorable Rev. Ralph Abernathy, that they remain peaceful. Some violence did break out—this was, after all, the turbulent year 1968—but I heard of no reports that tournament-goers ran into trouble. In his reference to the march, Bruce was really saying: Don't worry. Despite the march, the championships will still succeed.

Next Bruce writes about books. As I've mentioned, during my first visit to Bruce's home, I was most impressed with his martial arts book collection. All the walls of his study room were lined with nothing but martial arts and philosophy books. I had never seen so many martial arts books in one room. I remember spending hours with him searching for books in old book stores in Los Angeles, in Washington, D.C., and in Hong Kong. We'd make a day of it and even after we had roamed bookstore aisles for hours, he'd want to stay longer. He loved reading about a wide diversity of martial arts and philosophy subjects. As I've mentioned in the chapter about Bruce's early years, my friend studied philosophy in college and was one of the greatest martial arts philosophers. I'm happy I could contribute to his collection by giving him three books. Because he wanted to find more titles from Korea, I helped to add a few more titles to his shelves—all of which I'm sure he read cover-to-cover—but he was never fully satisfied. He always sought more.

59

In my taekwondo studios, we have always promoted the wealth of knowledge—or as we say to our students, "you need the muscles in the brain to match the muscles in the arms and legs." I tell my students that if you develop a habit of reading a book a week beginning at age 10—really not all that hard, especially if children shut off the TV and reject computer video games a few nights a week—you will have read 520 books by the time you turn 20. That's one reason why I respect the basketball coach Phil Jackson. He tells his adult players to read, and even assigns them books. They say Michael Jordan appreciated his coach's reading lists when Jackson was with the Chicago Bulls. And now, as

Letter Two

Jhoon,

Glad to hear that you will have Norris and Stone coming to your tournament. It will fill up the program nicely. Maybe you don't need Lewis.

At any rate, without the Poor People March, I'm sure with your knowledge and drive, the National Tournaments will be a success.

When you called, I forgot to ask you. You see, I'm a book collector. So far, I have three books on Korean Karate, all of which you gave me

(1) 跆拳拳法 — 朴哲熙 (2) 唐手道教本 — 黄琦

and (3) 跆拳道 — 崔泓熙.

Can you write to Korea and have someone send you some of the books on Karate and Judo, or anything on martial art. I'll reimburse you, when they arrive. Will you look into it? It will add much to my collections to make it more international.

My project is coming along very smoothly, and this Friday Sterling, Coburn and I will have another meeting. Things will turn out exactly as I planned.

Take Care

Bruce

P.S. What ever happened to the Characters 跆拳道 from Korea?

coach of the Los Angeles Lakers, Jackson has star center Shaquille O'Neal reading more. Bruce Lee and Phil Jackson would probably have gotten along well given their mutual interest in books, athleticism and Zen Buddhism.

Anyway, Bruce mentions a project and his meetings with actor James Coburn and Stirling Silliphant, an Academy Award-winning screenwriter—("In the Heat of the Night")—who became Bruce's main Hollywood mentor. That project is the movie "The Silent Flute." Although the real activity on the movie was still several months away, these were some of the initial meetings. Bruce was hoping to realize his dream of becoming a superstar through the film medium—a dream that he later did realize first in Hong Kong.

The Chinese characters at the bottom of this letter represent jeet kune do in Chinese.

Chapter Seven

Bruce Can Prove a
Point When Necessary

"Bruce was the strongest man I knew for his weight, and a great arm wrestler"
—Jhoon Rhee

In 1968, Stirling Silliphant arranged for Bruce to choreograph some fight scenes for his film "A Walk in a Spring Rain," which was shooting in Tennessee. This was a good decision because my friend had a certain skill for choreography; he knew what moves could dazzle an audience. It was also convenient for Silliphant, because it would allow Bruce to be on hand to continue Silliphant's three-times-a-week private instruction. But when Bruce arrived in Tennessee, personnel problems surfaced. Silliphant recounted the story to one of Bruce's biographers Robert Clouse:

> The two stuntmen on the picture, who were real Hollywood redneck types, wondered why I had brought this little Chinese guy along. They had never heard of

Bruce Lee, and who was this guy to teach them how to fight. '....We'll kick his ass.' Their attitude was very wrong, so I took them aside and told them that this little guy, pound for pound, could rip lions' asses, so you better not mess with him[12].

I was not there in Tennessee but I agree with Silliphant. Bruce was the strongest man I knew for his weight, and a great arm wrestler; I never saw him lose an arm-wrestling contest. I also question whether these thugs—and that's what they were, really—had truly never heard of Bruce. He was such a well-known guy then, and so I think these jerks were just trying to get in the news. This sort of situation is pretty dangerous for Bruce from a PR standpoint. If he really used a lot of force, he would lose by winning. There'd be a headline in the newspapers or at least in the trade-press magazines: "Bruce Lee Beats Up A Couple of Nobodies." By the way, I've never been challenged like this and I try to avoid such jerks. To avoid such altercations, I cast my three-year-old son in my "Nobody Bothers Me" ads to promote my martial arts studios. I reasoned that if I said it, thugs would inevitably try and prove themselves against me out on the street somewhere, and would try to create a situation where I couldn't walk away. Bruce and I talked about this danger to our careers— how we couldn't let ourselves get in a situation where we had to beat up or maim some stupid bully.

64

---

[12]Robert Clouse, *Bruce Lee: The Biography*, Unique Publications, Burbank, Calif., 1988, p. 70.

But Silliphant felt he needed to get these guys to pipe down. "I told them that we'd have to clear this thing up," he told Clouse, "because they'd be working for him and this wasn't going to help my film, so we'd better have a little demonstration. I didn't want anybody to get hurt, but I wanted to get a little respect for Bruce. So they said, 'Anything you want. Just give us a chance to show this little sonofa....'[13]

"So I told Bruce about it and he said, 'Ya gotta straighten these guys out. No problem.' They went out to the swimming pool where Bruce had an airbag and chose the biggest guy first and had him stand about three feet from the edge of the pool, brace himself and hold the bag for protection.

"Bruce said, 'What I'm going to do is stand right up in front of you and with no warning, no windup, no run, no nothing, I'm just going to kick. I'm going to hit the airbag you're holding, and you can get into any position you want to. I'll lift you from there out into the air and into the swimming pool!'

"So this guy gets into a kind of crouch, the two of them laughing when Bruce zapped him to catapult him nearly to the other side of the pool. He almost missed the water! The guy came up a Christian! Instant baptism! But the second guy wasn't convinced. He figured he was tougher than the first guy and it was

65

---

[13]Although this is a quote of what someone else said, I have left profanity out of my book, out of respect especially for young readers.

just a lucky punch. Some kind of Chinese magic. So, he really gets braced. I mean, he's like a linebacker. Bruce kicked and that sonofa… almost missed the other end of the pool. He was up in the air and gone. Those two became slaves of Bruce. Bruce loved it. He loved doing things like that."[14]

And I love this story. I wanted to share it with any of Bruce's fans who had not yet heard or read it. Bruce had a way of humbling those who needed to be humbled. I'm glad he didn't hurt them, but I do think the director did the right thing by asking Bruce to demonstrate his speed and power. Those guys might have been prejudiced against Asian-Americans. Bruce ran into some of that—especially because he married a white, American woman—but for the most part people did not discriminate against him or Linda.

66

Linda and Bruce each had a healthy, optimistic attitude toward people and gave everyone the benefit of the doubt. "I grew up in Seattle and attended schools that were very mixed—Asian-Americans, African-Americans, Hispanics and Jews," she recently told me. "I was quite accustomed to hanging out with different people. When Bruce and I got married and moved to Oakland, we didn't really encounter any discrimination. Of course, if you're not looking for acts of prejudice, you often don't see it. We had no major incidents. Bruce was not a person who considered himself less than anyone else because he was Chinese. He looked straight

---

[14]Clouse, p. 71.

across at people and did not expect to be looked down upon."
Linda reminded me of a story that I once told her and Bruce regarding this subject. She said I should share it in this book. Several years ago, after I made a substantial amount of money with my schools and other endeavors, my first wife and I decided we should buy this big, rather elegant house in a well-to-do neighborhood in suburban Washington. We had worked hard for it after all, and we needed the room for our family and our many guests. When I described the house to one of my staff members at the time—we always joked with each other—he said that the neighbors would think I'm just the Chinese houseboy for the real homeowners.

One Sunday after we'd settled into our new big home, I was mowing the spacious lawn and I saw that a Cadillac convertible driven by a well-dressed guy wearing sunglasses had pulled over to the curb next to our lawn. He was whistling, which I couldn't hear over the mower, but saw him waving his hands. I shut down the machine to ask what he wanted. He said, "Hey boy, how much do you charge an hour?" Obviously, he thought I was the hired help. I said, "Nothing, sir. But I get to share the master bedroom with the madam who owns the house." He drove off, shaking his head. Bruce and Linda were both amused at this story.

Even though Bruce didn't encounter much ethnic prejudice there were some people who didn't like his approach to martial arts. His unusual ideas and modification of traditional styles of

67

teaching had earned him quite a few enemies among other teachers of the martial arts in the United States. And Bruce was outspoken. He ridiculed their insistence on rigid adherence to traditional, ceremonial styles and stances. "The stances most students learn are worthless," he once said. "They are just too artificial and mechanical and don't prepare a student for actual combat. A guy could get clobbered while getting into his classical mess. Classical methods, which I consider a form of paralysis, only solidify what was once fluid. Their practitioners are merely blindly rehearsing systematic routines and stunts that will lead nowhere...So many instructors just want to push the same old buttons and get you to react the same old ways. Over and over. You are a man, not a robot."[15]

68

Bruce believed we are all free to express ourselves. He wasn't bound by tradition at all. He didn't teach any form, and he didn't believe in style. I debated him about that, because without form there is no identification about your expression. He didn't respond much to my argument, and he always respected my opinion. We could disagree and still be close friends. Bruce even scoffed at some of the martial arts' supposedly sacrosanct symbols. "If you like colored belts go look at a rainbow," he said. "I don't have a karate belt whatsoever. I think it might be useful to hold up your pants, but that's about it."[16] Again, you can see his wit here and know that he said that last line with a mischievous grin.

[15]Clouse, p. 70.
[16]Ibid.

In newspaper interviews and television appearances, Bruce was equally disdainful of the kung-fu establishment in Hong Kong. At one point, he appeared on a Hong Kong television talk show with several prominent kung-fu masters. One of the masters assumed a stance and challenged the others to push him out of position. One by one, the masters shoved and tugged at him, unable to budge him. Wearing a scornful almost mocking facial expression, he waited for Bruce to take his turn. Bruce got up from his chair, walked over and punched the supposedly immovable master in the face, knocking him off his feet and to the floor. Afterward, Bruce said, "Anybody can defend themselves if they dictate how they are going to be attacked."[17]

Now I don't condone this sort of action, but that was Bruce the Non-conformist being a bit sensational. And, you know it made for great TV. And while I don't agree with the actual punch he threw, I do agree with the message behind it. I don't care much for the rigid kung-fu establishment in Hong Kong, either. Some of the Hong Kong masters who created the art's foundations were from a farming background and didn't have an education or understanding of mechanics and physics, which I formally studied and which Bruce, with his incredible thirst for knowledge and perfection in his craft, came to understand as well. He and I often discussed the mechanics of martial arts. We

[17]Clouse, p. 71.

bounced around ideas—I was able to teach him a few things about physics—and he constantly stimulated me with his probing and always challenging intellect.

Chapter Eight
Letters Three and Four

"Martial arts is 99 percent philosophy and 1 percent action. Martial arts without philosophy is merely street fighting."
—Jhoon Rhee

Letter Three

In the last chapter, I end by mentioning Bruce bouncing around ideas. He had many great ideas! The two previous letters were examples of Bruce's undying interest in helping me and my career as well as sharing tidbits of his own professional life. In this next one, Bruce starts his correspondence with more martial arts business—or what I call "networking, 1960s' style." Back in the 1960s, the martial arts were still pretty new and widely misunderstood by the American public. We were pioneers struggling to promote our reputations, our careers and our arts to the masses. To help each other, we engaged in what we all know today as "networking." We shared personal and professional contacts to help one another in our pursuit of excellence. Keep this in mind as you read the first paragraph of this particular letter from Bruce.

Then, to my surprise, he abruptly changed the subject in his letter from business to philosophy. Bruce wrote me a poem, "Who Am I? and Which Are You?" that revealed his deeply reflective nature. How unusual, and how mature, for a person in his mid-20s. How revealing of the depth within the man, and his quest, and identification with those "who set their sights on the good, the admirable, the excellent, and believe they can achieve it."

Bruce Lee was a person of many dimensions. No wonder he was a legend in his own time. I wasn't as much of a philosopher then as now. When I first received Bruce's letter and read his poem I recall thinking, "How profoundly thoughtful. My friend really has what it takes not only to be successful, but to leave a powerful and positive legacy in this world."

For me, a legacy only matters to the extent that someone truly makes a positive difference in people's lives. Bruce was doing just that. He had a vehicle—martial arts—through which he could dedicate himself to mind/body excellence and bring his uplifting spirit into people's lives. Then he set out to capture the most powerful communications medium of the age—movies. Bruce was never just some guy performing incredible physical feats. He was this, of course, but also much more. His much deserved fame is because of the inner man expressing himself through the external form of his art.

After all, "Who am I?" is one of the instinctual cosmic questions we, as human beings, ponder in life. Understanding who we are, or at least trying to answer the question, is critical in the search for deciphering human consciousness and is the foundation for many of the world's religious and spiritual principles. Many of Bruce's letters are truly extraordinary in their degree of emotional depth and philosophical substance. It is not easy to convey, in just one "first draft," a powerful message that motivates, inspires and intimately connects; it usually requires several rewritten drafts and an intense effort to communicate just the right thoughts. Yet Bruce dashed this off in one sitting.

73

I recall reading and ruminating over Bruce's words. He contributed to my own active quest to understand the human condition, and my determination to make a positive difference in the lives of others—especially children and families. And as I've advanced in my years, I have also gained a degree of passion and felt a certain ability to set an example for seniors of how active and vibrant life beyond age 60 can be.

Perhaps, then, this is a very good place to share a slice or two of my own world view. I've had the benefit of more than 30 years of

Letter Three

Jhoon Goo,

Enclosed find Norris' Ad. This is the most recent one. I'll try to save them for you in the future. Also, I have included other ads of similar nature which might be of help.

WHO AM I?

Who am I?
That is the age-old question
Asked by every man
At one time or another.
Though he looks into a mirror
And recognizes the face,
Though he knows his own name
And age and history,
Still he wonders, deep down,
Who am I?

Am I a giant among men,
Master of all I survey,
Or an ineffectual pygmy
Who clumsily blocks his own way?
Am I the self-assured gentleman
With a winning style,
The natural born leader
Who makes friends instantly,
Or the frightened heart
Tiptoeing among strangers,
Who, behind a frozen smile, trembles
Like a little boy lost in a dark forest?
Most of us yearn to be one,
But fear we are the other.

Yet we CAN be
What we aspire to be.
Those who cultivate
Their natural instincts,
Who set their sights
On the good, the admirable, the excellent,
And believe they can achieve it

Letter Three

Will find their confidence rewarded.
And, in the process,
They will discover the true identity
Of him who looks back from the mirror.

WHICH ARE YOU?

The doubters said,
"Man cannot fly,"
The doers said,
"Maybe, but we'll try,"
And finally soared
Into the morning's glow.
While non-believers
Watched from below.

The doubters claimed
The world was flat,
Ships plunged over its edge.
And that was that!
Yet a brand new world
Some doers found,
And returned to prove
This planet round.

The doubters knew
'Twas fact, "Of course,
No noisy gadget
Would e'er replace the horse."
Yet the carriages
Of doers, sans equine,
Came to traverse
All our roads in time.

But those who kept saying
"It can't be done,"
Never are the victories
Or the honors won;
But, rather,
By the believing, doing kind,
While the doubters
Watched from far behind.

Letter Three

In conclusion may I warn you that negativeness very often unknowingly creeps up upon us. It helps occasionally to stop all thoughts (the chattering of worries, anticipation, etc. in your head) and then once more refreshingly march bravely on. Just as the maintaining of good health may require the taking of unpleasant medicine, so the condition of being able to do the things we enjoy often requires the performance of a few we don't. Remember my friend that it is not what happens that counts, it is how you react to them. You have what it takes. I know you will win out one way or the other. So damn the torpedo, full speed ahead! Remember what this Chinaman says. "Circumstances? Hell! I make circumstances!"

Peace and inner harmony
Bruce

*But those who keep saying
"It can't be done,"
Never are the victories
Or the honors won;
But, rather,
By the believing, doing kind,
While the doubters
Watched from far behind.*

In conclusion may I warn you that negativeness very often unknowingly creep up upon us. It helps occasionally to stop all thoughts (the chattering of worries, anticipation, etc. in your head) and then once more refreshingly march bravely on. Just as the maintaining of good health may require the taking of unpleasant medicine, so the condition of being able to do the things we enjoy often require the performance of a few we don't. Remember my friend that it is not what happens that count, it is how you react to them. You have what it takes. I know you will win out one way or the other. So damn the torpedo, full speed ahead! Remember what this Chinaman says "Circumstances? Hell! I make circumstances!"

*Peace and inner harmony
Bruce*

life experience beyond what Bruce had due to his tragic and early death. Bruce's bright flame was a like a comet. Whereas with me, my world view has developed through the accumulation of nearly 70 years—more than 40 of them involved with children's education and the establishment of a system worldwide for personal growth and development for people of all ages. I am compiling my philosophy of life into a little book to be titled *Simple Truths*.

During the 1980s and 1990s, I had set myself an important goal, based on my philosophy: To change our society by applying the principles of martial arts discipline to the wider educational system. There are seven qualities that one must attain to be a champion in the martial arts, and those qualities all have counterparts in our life outside the school. Those qualities, and their counterparts in life, are: speed (alertness); endurance (perseverance); timing (punctuality); power (knowledge); balance (rationality); flexibility (gentleness); and posture (honesty). Martial arts is 99 percent philosophy and 1 percent action. Martial arts without philosophy is merely street fighting.

77

Letter Four

After Bruce attended my tournament in 1968, I called to thank him for once again lending his dynamic presence, his exhilarating spirit and his big-draw name—all of which helped make the event a success. During one of our late-night talk-eat-and-workout sessions, I'd spoken at some length with him about a promising new project I'd been considering. A few months earlier, in April 1968, one of the local television producers on Washington's Channel 5 called me to talk about creating a self-defense show for a television series. The producer was very interested in producing the "Jhoon Rhee Self-Defense TV Show." I got excited at the prospect of spreading martial arts through television.

When the producer called, the first person who came to my mind was Bruce Lee because of his experience playing Kato in "The Green Hornet" and his appearances on other TV shows. I called Bruce right away and told him about it. When he came to Washington in June we had more time to discuss the possible show. Bruce was happy for me and, ever-generous with his ideas, offered me some good suggestions.

I knew that Bruce's time was extremely valuable. In 1968, he was charging $250.00 an hour to teach private lessons to Steve McQueen, James Coburn, and a few other celebrities. I appreciated his willingness to help me, his friend, without hesitation and without charging me for his precious advice.

As you will see in his letter, Bruce was articulate, organized, thoughtful, and very responsible with his suggestions. First, he proposed detailed ideas for the program's background, costumes, and situations. Notice how he was looking out for my

Jhoon Goo,

Here are some thoughts that enter my mind after our phone conversation

BACKGROUND FOR PROGRAM

A) Light Oriental background music which becomes louder before and after program
B) The setting has to be simple Oriental design with mats and all—most important your own school emblem (big!) in the background

COSTUMES

A) You the head instructor wear gi at all time
B) The lady wears different street clothes

SITUATION

A) Realistic duplication of actual attack
(Note: whoever the attacker, he must be fierce and rough toward his victim)
B) Provide props as much as possible to capture the street scene—like chair, phony car, etc. etc.

LESSONS

1) Take one technique at a time and show it from different angles and perspectives so as not to make the lesson monotonous
2) Needless to say, the program has to be both educational and entertaining…Realize the fact that too educational will make the show too dull; on the other hand, too entertaining will decrease the martial art spirit. However, though a happy medium is desired, for a TV program, do lean toward showmanship.
3) Besides your usual lesson plans, do give brief lectures on safety at home, in a car, walking alone on the street, etc. etc.

4) Do take advantage of current paper clippings of attacks so as to instill fear that will lead to taking actual lessons. Get as much statistics as you can on crimes, attacks, etc. and report it on the air.

5) Definitely encourage the viewer to write in.

Letter Four

79

Letter Four

6) As the program goes on, you should sell some of your product….books, or whatever items you feel would help the ladies.

SOMETHING TO BE CONSIDERED

1) You must secure ownership of your film pilot no matter [if] it sells or not.

2) Make your program a package deal with you as the hiring force for whatever assistance you have on the show

3) I would recommend—if it does not conflict with policy—that you have the girl plus the attackers so that you become the principle of the show while those two are demonstrators. Of course, you will occasionally demonstrate on the attacker as to the proper and correct way of execution.

4) Have lawyer consult the screen guild as to union's policy on your type of show. Do this when concrete deal is being made.

What more can I say at this time but to wish you the best and hope the show will materialize. Should I come up with more ideas, I'll write you. See if you can make pilot here in the West Coast. I should be of help.

COSTUMES

A). you the head instructor wear gi at all time

B) the lady wear different street clothes

SITUATION

A). Realistic duplication of actual attack
(NOTE:- whoever the attacker, he must be fierce and rough toward the victim)

B). provide props as much as possible to capture the street scene — like chair, phony car, etc etc.

interests by telling me to make sure my school's emblem is featured prominently on the set. Why miss an opportunity to advertise?! When I re-read this letter while writing this book, I was reminded again of how he cared about me and my career, at every twist and turn. Notice how he recommended how to film the lessons and how to connect the shows to my school and to product promotions like my books and martial arts-related accessories. Bruce taught me a lot about marketing myself. We often talked about the challenge of promoting your career without coming across as boastful and self-centered. We always told ourselves that the way to avoid that perception was to remain as dignified and humble as possible, which also fits into each of our personal philosophies. Finally, Bruce gave me some sound advice about how to protect the legal rights to the completed pilot film, whether or not it sold to the TV station.

81

When I presented my program outline of the TV show, the producer was very pleased with the thorough plan. We did produce one pilot film, which was a challenge to me because I never knew about the film production business. The students who participated in the pilot were my veteran students in the late 1960s: Mrs. Marian Hobson played a female victim and Mr. Jim Martin played an attacker. I was an instructor for the TV audience. The show did not fly, as they say in Hollywood. But it sure was an interesting experience.

Chapter Nine

Letters Five Through Ten; Bruce Struggles With Ailing Project Yet Our Friendship Grows

"My first love is martial art. By martial art, I mean an unrestricted athletic expression of an individual soul."
—Bruce Lee

As Letter Three (the poetry correspondence) demonstrates, Bruce constantly sought knowledge and understanding. He goes further into this approach in the following passage from Linda's biography of her husband:

I am learning to understand rather than immediately judge or be judged. I cannot blindly follow the crowd and accept their approach. I will not allow myself to indulge in the usual manipulating game of role creation. Fortunately for me, my self-knowledge has transcended that and I have come to understand that life is best to be lived and not to be conceptualized. I am happy because I am daily growing and am honestly not knowing where the limit lies. To be certain, every day can be a revelation or a new discovery. I treasure the memory of the past misfortunes. It has added more to my bank of fortitude.

My first love is martial art. By martial art, I mean an unrestricted athletic expression of an individual soul. Martial art also means daily hermit-like physical training to upgrade or maintain one's quality. To live is to express one's self freely in creation. Creation, I must say, is not a fixed something or a solidification. So I hope my fellow martial artists will open up and be transparently real and I wish them well in their own process of finding their cause. [18]

84

To achieve these goals, Bruce knew he needed the tools of his trade—the martial arts and acting. So in early 1969, Bruce, James Coburn and Stirling Silliphant began formally working on creating a film vehicle for Bruce. As you recall, Bruce had already met with the two earlier for a brainstorming session. Bruce wrote a treatment, a writer was hired, and the three waited eagerly for a draft script. Unfortunately, the writer came up with a film that was far from the original treatment, and the three principals were disappointed. They decided to write the film themselves, and met three afternoons a week for several months to work diligently on "The Silent Flute."

Stirling Silliphant described the message behind the film this way: "'The Silent Flute' is the call of the heart, the call of the soul, and only certain people can hear it. Bruce would appear at different times in

---

[18]Lee, p. 171.

the story and he would be playing this flute, and you couldn't hear it, but monkeys could hear it, and different creatures could hear it, and by the end of the story the American guy, who is on the quest, hears it. And once he hears it he begins to achieve perfection. But in this quest there is a great deal of wonderful combat."[19]

When it was finished, they sent the script to Warner Brothers. The studio liked it, but conditioned their support on the film's being shot in India for financial reasons. The three men went so far as to spend three blisteringly hot weeks in India scouting locations and looking for martial arts students to use as extras, but the project ultimately failed when the studio decided that it couldn't be made in India after all. Bruce went back to teaching and the occasional television appearance, struggling with money problems and Hollywood's indifference.

85

Letter Five

During all the machinations of "The Silent Flute," Bruce wrote me several letters, and we saw each other a couple of times, including a visit I made to their house in Los Angeles. Bruce and Linda had just bought their first house, after a few years of renting various houses and apartments in the L.A. area. Linda was pregnant with Shannon and the couple began to think they needed a house of their own even though they were initially reluctant

---

[19]Clouse, p. 84.

to take the plunge into home ownership. They looked around and eventually found a steal-of-a-deal in Bel Air. After consulting with Bruce's friend and student Steve McQueen, who knew the area's real estate market, and his business manager, they realized they'd be wise to snap up the $47,000 home. Bruce wasn't wealthy—despite his fame—but he wanted to be in Bel Air, for one reason to be close to his celebrity students.

In talking with Linda recently, she recalled many memories about their first home. "We moved to the Bel Air house in late 1968," she told me.

We got talked into buying the house. People kept telling us we were throwing away all this money on rent. But you have to make enough money to afford the payments so we bought a place that was kind of a fixer-upper and when we sold it, it was still a fixer-upper because we didn't have enough money to fix it up the way we wanted. The great thing about that house is that it had a large flat backyard, unlike many houses in Bel Air. It had a patio with eaves over it where all the punching bags were hung. We always had a houseful of guys working out in the backyard.

Bruce also had an office in the house where he had all his thousands of books and a desk and some workout equipment. He had a bench for doing ab work and dumbbells for forearm work. I remember he'd spend hours with you, Jhoon, in the office—especially in the evening after working out all day—to talk about all kinds of martial arts and philosophy. You guys would also watch boxing films. Bruce had a projector and a collection of boxing films. He'd buy them from *Ring* magazine.

I recall those old films; many of them were of boxing matches from the 1930s and 40s. Some of the old-time fighters fought very primitively. They didn't guard their chins and ribs. Their arms would stick out away from their bodies like street fighters. They weren't fast, and they didn't look like boxers. Bruce and I would make jokes and laugh at some of those guys.

When I returned home from Los Angeles, I sent Brandon, who was a couple of months shy of four at that time, a stuffed bear as a token of appreciation for the Lees' hospitality during my stay with them. So you see in Letter Five that Bruce thanked me for sending the bear. I've thought a lot about Brandon in recent months. When he was a little boy, he was very independent. In fact, he was self-reliant and sometimes hard to connect with. But when he was 19, he came to see me in Washington, which surprised me because he was never so friendly when he was a little boy, and I hadn't seen him since he was about seven. But I always loved him and bought him toys. In about 1980 when he came to Washington, he said, "I just wanted to see you." I took him to a Korean restaurant and we talked a lot. His personality was much different than his father's. Bruce was active all the time, cracked jokes constantly and seemed to always have something to say. Brandon was calmer than his dad. The son did resemble the father. They were both very striking in appearance and I'm sure got a lot of looks from the ladies.

As we all know, Bruce Lee was very conscious not only of his physical abilities, but also of his physical appearance. Whenever I visited his home, I was reminded of his small daily discipline to build muscles in his arms and legs. He didn't have big muscles in his legs, but they were very solid. He had fairly large muscles on his arms, his chest and his shoulders. Bruce never had an idle moment. He was always doing something with his hands to develop his forearms or stretching or punching and kicking. I asked Linda during that visit, "Is he like that—all day long?" She replied, "Almost always." Even when he was eating he would exercise his wrists. I wouldn't be surprised if he trained in his sleep!

In my thank you letter, I asked Bruce to offer his suggestions for the best way to build muscle mass on my arms and upper body. I always had good muscles in my legs, but not in my upper body. So in his return letter, he recommended that I order and start taking food supplements and also add beef-up ingredients to the protein drinks. As you can tell from what he wrote, Bruce really was cordial and sincere in trying to help me get what I wanted. I followed his instruction very seriously and, indeed, I did get bigger. In one of my tournaments, in 1970, I performed a demonstration with my shirt off just to show my newly acquired musculature to my students and the audience. I motivated many of my instructors and students through that demonstration, and almost everybody started getting into bodybuilding. So again, we thank you, Bruce.

俊九先生.

Thank you for your wonderful gift to my son; he sleeps with the bear nowadays.

Enclosed I'm rushing the ad & information where you can obtain the gain weights food supplements. Be sure to order it from York, Pa., instead of from Los Angeles, Calif. As there is a difference in postage.

Add peanuts, eggs (with shells) and bananas into the powder with milk and mix them in a blender. If you really want faster result use 'half and half' instead of ordinary milk.

The postman is here. I better mail this.

Talk to you later.

Your friend,
Bruce Lee

Letter Five

89

Enclosed I'm rushing the ad & information where you can obtain the gain weights food supplement. Be sure to order it from york, Pa. instead of from Lo Angeles, Calf. as there is a difference in postage.

Add peanuts. eggs (with shells) and ~~bananas~~ bananas into the powder ~~and~~ with milk and mix them in a blender. If you really want faster result use 'half and half' instead of ordinary milk

The postman is here I better mail this

Talk to you later

Your friend
Bruce Lee

Letter Six

In this letter, Bruce is a little frustrated with his movie career and the foot-dragging on "The Silent Flute," as you can see with his mention of changing agents. He didn't switch at that time, as I recall, because he realized his agent was doing all he could. Bruce also writes about "The Green Hornet" re-runs, and I remember feeling happy that big-market TV stations were re-running episodes of the series because that meant Bruce was getting royalties, which he and his family needed. Finally, he notes that at this period of time he is teaching all three of the American martial art stars. He took great pride in that.

Letter Seven

Although Bruce had a hectic schedule in the late spring of 1969, he put everything on hold—including the activity around "The Silent Flute"—to be my special guest at the 1969 Jhoon Rhee National Championships. Bruce performed a demonstration, to the typically super-receptive audience, and also joined a few U.S. senators in presenting the trophies to the winners in the finals. Our photographers took a lot of shots of Bruce, as they usually did when he attended the tournaments. The pictures he refers to in Letter Six were photos of that event.

Letter Six

Jhoon,

Glad to hear a representative of Black Belt will come for your interview. I hope it will be a good one.

No wonder you couldn't get in touch with me. You have the phone number mixed up. Instead of 883-0241, the correct number is 838-0241.

No news yet from the movie world. The Green Hornet is having re-run every-day at 6 in L.A. I understand New York T.V. station also run the Hornet show everyday. I'm planning to change agent soon as this present one is not doing too much.

I've been busy training and working on my book. Besides Norris, Mike Stone also take lesson from me now.

Do give my regards to your wife.

Take Care

Bruce

Letter Seven

Jhoon Goo,
Received letter and pictures this morning.

I do believe that frequent letters to Mito during production stage would help. You keep him up to date of your plan while in the meantime implant your idea of protective equipment in his mind. I feel your improvement of the old plus lower cost would attract Jim, Mito's brother.

Enclosed find some characters that I've written. I talked to you on this when I was in D.C. Would you have the gentleman write it for me, except this time sideways instead of up and down. The measurement will be. Length: 5 1/2 ft width: 14 in.

My mother and my younger brother are arriving from Hong Kong tomorrow morning.

Take Care

Bruce

As I've mentioned, Bruce Lee always promoted me, as well as my five taekwondo books, the movie I starred in, and my safety equipment, which I'll explain below. He was working with Mito Uyehara to publish my books through Mito's company, Ohara Publications. Jim Uyehara is Mito's younger brother who took over the martial arts supply company, while Mito oversaw the publishing part of the business. Bruce introduced me to Jim to market my safety equipment the next year in 1970.

Bruce reminded me to stay in close touch with the Uyehara brothers, so that they would continue to be aware of my equipment ideas. Bruce always told me that when people are busy, out of sight means out of mind. Furthermore, he would talk about the high quality and fair price of my products to anyone he thought could help me.

93

Now about my safety equipment. Earlier I had mentioned that in the late 1960s I had some concerns about the inherently violent nature of my craft—thoughts that led to my development of martial arts ballet. During those years, as taekwondo and other martial arts became more popular, I saw a number of people injured in training or, more often, in the heat of competition. At a 1969 championship tournament, for example, one of my students took a hard kick to his face, breaking his cheekbone. I came away from that tournament feeling bad for my student and determined to do something to reduce the frequency and severity of martial arts-related injuries.

In addition, one of my goals has always been to broaden the appeal of the martial arts as much as possible. Consequently, I developed Jhoon Rhee Safe-T equipment, protective gear that cover the "weapons"—the hands and feet—and the head, which allows full-contact training without the risk of serious injury. The gear was originally based on the design of a padded water skiing jacket. No one had worn safety gear before I invented it, and I believe it has changed the complexion of martial arts for the better. It's done much to remove the stigma of brutality from the martial arts, and has made it possible to attract many more women and children as students. I'm certain of one thing: If, in 1969, my student had worn this equipment, he may have been bruised but he wouldn't have broken any bones. In the mid-80s, my son Jimmy and my cousin Sunny took over the management and ownership of the company I started. They've done a great job, providing top-notch products with a profitable operation year after year.

Of course, I've had lots of help in marketing my safety gear. Soon after I launched my company, Joe Lewis and a friend of his wrote an article about the equipment and had the story published in *Parade* magazine. Then, in 1973 Joe spread the word even further. "I went on national TV, 'The Merv Griffin Show,' and I was doing a [martial arts] demonstration," Joe recently recalled. "Jhoon had just developed some new safety equipment called Safe-T Chop, which I was wearing. After the demo, Merv asked what I was wearing, I said, 'This is new equipment developed by a man in

Washington, D.C. named Jhoon Rhee.' When Jhoon heard about what I said, he sent me [an unsolicited] $1,000."

Around this same time, in 1973, my safety gear got another marketing boost from an unexpected place. Howard Jackson had just become the country's top-ranked karate champion. (Howard was the first African-American in karate history to be rated number one in his sport, and from the 1980s to the present, he has worked as Chuck Norris' assistant.) A young black belt and writer, John Corcoran, had just been hired by Mito Uyehara to work at *Black Belt* magazine. John wrote a cover story about Howard Jackson, with a cover photo of him wearing my Safe-T-Punch equipment. (See U.S. Patent in Appendix). As a result, my safety equipment sales increased dramatically. I called John and thanked him, and ever since he and I have shared a close personal and professional friendship.

95

Back to Bruce's letter. I knew a famous calligrapher in Korea named Mr. Kim. He had written the characters of "jeet kune do" and bordered them in a beautiful vertical frame, as diagrammed in Bruce's letter. Bruce, however, wanted it placed in a horizontal frame, which he instructed in this letter.

Finally, Bruce mentions that his mother and younger brother Robert, a singer, were arriving in Los Angeles from Hong Kong the next morning. He was always excited to see them and showed them a lot of love.

Letter Eight

When Bruce next wrote to me, again in June 1969, he, Jim Coburn and Stirling Silliphant were deep into their work on "The Silent Flute." Bruce had high hopes for the script and waited patiently for a long time as it went through various stages of development. In his letter, he expressed his impatience at the slow deliberations of the project's progress.

When Bruce was hot on an idea, he wanted it to materialize immediately. In some ways, he was like a kid who can't wait for Christmas and chooses to peek at his gifts before the Big Day. I can understand this trait in my friend. He came to every project with all-out enthusiasm, and foot-dragging has a way of making that exuberance wane. I was disappointed for him that "The Silent Flute" suffered setback after setback and still wish that it could have been produced with Bruce as the star. During his impatient and eventually fruitless wait, Bruce heard from Hong Kong's Raymond Chow, who owned Golden Harvest Productions. Chow offered Bruce a movie deal, and this marked the beginning of Bruce's new life in Hong Kong, which I'll chronicle in subsequent pages.

In the third paragraph of this letter, Bruce writes about his car accident—a minor one—and makes an inside joke: "It seemed that someone was pressing on my gas pedal." Let me fill you in. During my visit to Bruce's home in Bel Air, we were driving his

Jhoon,

I meant to have lunch with Mito today, but last minute deal came up so I had to cancel my plan. I should see him next week as he wants me to do an article for him.

Two days ago we had a meeting again on our movie project. Jim and I are getting impatient. Stirling thinks that we should have a final treatment two weeks from now. From that we will come to a decision and present the story to the studio and make it official.

Last week I had an accident on my Porsche, nothing serious, just bang it up on the left side. One thing though, it seemed that someone was pressing on my gas pedal….

Still haven't heard from the typewriter people. Maybe you should get in touch with them to find out what's going on. It will at least let us know what's what.

Bob Wall gave me a "giant" heavy bag. Weighing around 300 lb.—HERE I COME!! Working out more and more now. Delgado came over twice to work out. Too busy to teach though. He definitely wants to learn. He's opening a school tying in with Chuck Norris.

That's all for now.

Take Care

Bruce

Letter Eight

97

sporty red Porsche around the hills of L.A. on a beautiful, carefree Sunday. Bruce was driving a little too fast on the winding, narrow roads; he liked to feel the car hug the curves. But I was really not interested in feeling the car perform as only a Porsche can. O.K., that's an understatement. I was experiencing white-knuckled, teeth-clenching, chest-tightening fear. I could barely talk, I was so nerve-wracked, and at one point after speeding through a tight turn, I told Bruce I thought he was driving too fast.

"Hey, I thought you were having fun and being a dare devil," he said. I asked him why he thought that, and he pointed out that my foot was pressing down on top of his on the gas pedal. I couldn't believe it! I was unconsciously pressing down hard on the floor (the way you do when you're scared at someone else's driving) and, because the car was so small with the seats so close, my foot instead had found its way to the accelerator. I then released my grip, moved my foot to the passenger side of the car and it slowed down—mercifully. Bruce teased me about that for a long, long time. I do admit, that once my hair stopped standing on end that it was indeed funny.

It wasn't unusual for Bruce to tease me or any of his friends. Although I understood that Bruce meant no harm—I knew it was all in good fun—others may not have. Here's what martial arts superstar Joe Lewis recently told me: "Bruce Lee had a tendency to make fun of other people's accomplishments," Joe recalled. "He'd make comments as if it were his harmless way of showing affection. But because he had a high self-esteem and strong inner self-confidence, he automatically projected that same strength on other people, even if others didn't have that confidence. As you know, it's the way intelligent people spar with each other. They make sarcastic comments, knowing that the intention is strictly fun. He'd tease me, saying I wasn't very smart. He'd say, 'Chuck Norris is a good kicker but he's so stiff.' He'd make fun of Mike Stone saying, 'Mike's fast but he's out of control. He's like a crazy man.' And I know he teased you, too, Jhoon. You had no immunity. Bruce liked to joke a lot. But he didn't realize that, unfortunately, many martial artists attach their self-esteem to their martial arts prowess. So if you make fun of their martial arts skills, they'd take it as making fun of them as a person. I recognize that in Bruce because I'm the same way."

99

I might add that if Bruce ever felt that he had hurt someone's feelings through his relentless teasing, he'd find a way to make the person feel better.

Anyway, in this letter Bruce made a reference to a "heavy" bag. If you visited the Lee's home at that time, the first thing that would catch your attention was a huge kicking bag weighing about 300 pounds. This bag was given to Bruce as a gift by my good friend Bob Wall, one of the co-stars in "Enter the Dragon." Bruce used the bag almost every day.

Finally, Bruce mentioned Mr. Louis Delgado, who was one of the best martial artists on the East Coast in the late 1960s. He moved to Los Angeles to open a martial arts studio connected with the Chuck Norris Studios. Unfortunately, a few years later I was told that Mr. Delgado died at a relatively young age. I never found out the cause of his death.

Letter Nine

Bruce wrote to me once again in June 1969. While this letter may lack the passion and humor of the others, it demonstrates—perhaps more than all the other letters—Bruce's commitment to helping promote my career. In this instance, Bruce had talked to Mito Uyehara, the publisher of *Black Belt* magazine, about my five-volume taekwondo book series, which was eventually published and has been available to the public for the last 30 years. Generally, martial artists are exceedingly loyal to their own style and tend to be prejudiced against those who practice other styles. Not Bruce. He was always happy to see my name and my discipline appear in magazines. Again, this embodies both true friendship and Bruce's self-confidence; he was not threatened by another master, me, and my genre.

Someone recently asked me if I ever felt that I was competing with Bruce or vice versa. I said that I did not. After all, our professional directions went in different ways. I was most interested in expanding my organization and Bruce was more interested in tutoring private

June 25, 1969

Jhoon,

Had lunch with Mito this afternoon. At a glance, I can see you are mentioned in both the upcoming B.B. and the new Karate Illustrated (a picture of you awarding a belt to Skipper in the Mullin story). The National has good "pictorial coverage" and I think "Letter to Editor" mentions your branch in Dominican Republic—so, all in all, good coverage, especially the National. Also, I talked to Mito about your book. I told him it will be of "quality" and he definitely likes to look over it. Well, I have bridged the gap. The rest is up to you. You can call him directly if you like.

Remember the article you sent me on kicking? Well, that was not enough, but they want to do it now with eight people or somewhere around that, like Oshima, Ark Yu Wong (the cripple!), Sea Choi, some Okinawa instructor, etc. etc. The topic will be on the various kicks, the side, the round house, the heel, etc. etc. Anyway, if in your discussion with Mito on your book prove to be successful, you might be able to come out to do the article and "represent" Tae Kwon Do, or the Korean version of the kicking. It will be a prestiges moment with the various representatives and also to establish you as the spokesman for the Korean style. Personally, I have all the confidence in your backing up the kicking quality with any of them present.

Anyway, give me a call and let me know how your discussion with Mito comes out.

Bruce

Jhoon,   June 25 1969

Had lunch with Mito this afternoon. At a glance, I can see you are mentioned in both the upcoming B.B. and the new Karate Illustrated (a picture of you awaring a belt to skipper in the mullin story). The National has good "pictorial Coverage" and I think "letter to Editor" mentions your branch in Dominican Republic ------ so, all in all, good Coverage, especially the National.

Letter Nine

101

students. He didn't like organized martial arts styles. He felt everyone should be free to express his or her own style. He was doing that.
I told him that to make history and expose the world to this wonderful discipline, you have to organize and expand to really make some
impact, and I felt my schools were doing just that. He was thinking
he could make his own impact through the movies, which he did. So
we had no sense of competition. He was a Chinese martial artist and
I am a Korean martial artist. I respected his whole person, him as
a human being and as a martial artist. And that respect was mutual.
What's more, we never seriously sparred. As those who follow martial arts know, it's really a courtesy of Oriental martial artists, especially among masters, to refrain from sparring because, if you do tan-
gle, friction could develop. It's OK, however, for a couple of first-
degree black belt artists to just share individual kicks and punches
and play around a little. And Bruce and I did that on many occasions.

Linda recently answered the same question about competitiveness
this way: "Bruce and Jhoon regarded themselves as equals. They
didn't have the same goals, and they had a different type of relationship than Bruce had with Chuck Norris or Joe Lewis, because these
guys came to Bruce wanting to learn and improve their fighting style.
They had a student/teacher relationship whereas Jhoon and Bruce
had a teacher/teacher relationship, one built on mutual respect."

Bruce mentioned the Dominican Republic in this letter because he
knew that I had more than 25 studios in that country and also real-

ized I wanted those studios to get some attention. He was explaining that they were discussed in a letter to the editor in *Karate Illustrated* magazine.

Bruce ended the letter with a reference to an article I wrote. One day, Bruce had called to inform me that Mito was interested in doing an article about kicking techniques of all the different martial arts—kung-fu, karate, taekwondo, etc. Bruce believed that I should be the spokesman for taekwondo. So he asked me to send my article on kicking as soon as possible. Bruce knew that my English still needed improvement and he wanted to help edit my article before giving it to Mito. I sent my completed article to Bruce. I had worked very hard on it and had high hopes that he would find it well-written. He didn't. I had to spend another week rewriting the article, and Bruce patiently waited.

103

In his letter, Bruce also talked about Tsutomu Ohshima, Sea Oh Choi and others, who were very active martial artists at the time. Master Ohshima is the karate master from Shotokan, Master Choi is one of the most respected hapkido masters at that time.

Letter Ten

Bruce wrote me one more letter in 1969, in November, and, once again, you can see that Bruce always promoted me to Mito; he didn't think it was right for a person to blow his own horn. Whenever I needed some help from *Black Belt* Bruce always said, "Don't worry, I will take care of it." And he always did. Here, Bruce was paving the way for me to meet Mito's brother Jim so that I might work with Jim in marketing my safety equipment. Bruce would subsequently introduce me to Jim, as I mentioned earlier.

The letter also shows Bruce's compassion as well. He wrote this after my national championships, which didn't go as well as we'd have liked. Turnout was down that year. This isn't to say the event was a flop, it wasn't. Still, I was disappointed and Bruce, being the perceptive man he was, picked up on my emotions. He hoped to lift my spirits and, through his kind words, I did feel better. This letter is also representative of Bruce's proclivity to add meaning to experience. He waxed philosophical and challenged me to consider the 1969 tournament a "stepping stone" and not a "stumbling block."

Jhoon Goo,

Just had lunch with Mito this afternoon. I have further sold him on the value of your chest protector. Subltely(sic), I have fed him with ideas on the protector and I'm pretty sure he has a favorable attitude even before he has seen the merchandise. Mito, as you probably know, now handles only the magazine. His brother Jim handles the mail order business. However, I have made suggestion for him to talk personally to you first. When things are agreed upon you can then transact arrangements with Jim. Mito would be the person to start, and he does have a most favorable attitude toward you. More than once he has remarked that he likes you.

Anyway, I just want to let you know how things are, and also I like you to know that the 1969 National was a stepping stone and not a stumbling block. Your mental attitude determines what you make of it, as stepping stone or stumbling block. Remember no man is really defeated unless he is discouraged.

As a side observer, I know you have done your part right, and though the outcome of the tournament was not quite up to standard, you did everything right. It is not what happens that is success or failure, but what it does to the heart of man.

You have that quality of being active, awake, pushing ahead at all times, and always ahead of the other tournament directors in terms of services, knowledge, and truthfulness. The last quality, I feel, definitely demands co-operation from your fellow colleagues. I wrote this not because I am cheering you up, maybe I am, but I want you to know that when the mean is in order, the end is ultimately inevitable. What you must not do now is to worry and think of the National that is now of the past. What you HABITUALLY THINK largely determines what you will ultimately become. Remember, success is a journey, not a destination. I have faith in your ability. You will do just fine.

Take Care

Bruce Lee

105

Anyway, I just want to let you know how things are, and also. I like you to know that the 1969 national was a stepping stone and not a stumbling block. Your mental attitude determine what you make of it, as stepping stone or stumbling block. Remember no man is really defeated unless he is discouraged.

Jhoon Rhee and Bruce Lee prepare to present the winner's trophy at the 1967 Jhoon Rhee National Championships.

Jhoon Rhee performs a high jump sidekick toward Danny Inosanto, one of Bruce Lee's loyal students.

Muhammad Ali and Jhoon Rhee discuss the Accupunch in Tokyo on June 27, 1976, before Ali's match with Antonio Inoki, the Japanese wrestler.

Bruce Lee and Jhoon Rhee appear on television in the Dominican Republic in 1970.

Bruce Lee and Jhoon Rhee spar together in Palos Verdes, California, in 1969, with Jhoon Rhee performing a side kick.

Jhoon Rhee performs a round kick with Bruce Lee as sparring opponent in Palos Verdes, California, in 1969.

An autographed picture from Bruce Lee to Jhoon Rhee.

To a friend, Jhoon Rhee.
Peace, Love, Brotherhood,
Bruce Lee

Bruce Lee and Jhoon Rhee spar together in Palos Verdes, California, in 1969, with Bruce Lee performing a side kick.

At the 1967 Jhoon Rhee National Championships, (front row from the left) Jhoon Rhee; Joe Lewis, the winner; Bruce Lee; Miss Maryland 1966 Ros Elaine Zetter; and John Wooley, second place winner and now the CEO of Schlotzky's Delicatessens.

Muhammad Ali and Jhoon Rhee take part in an open car parade before over one million people in Seoul, Korea on June 28, 1976.

Bruce Lee and Jhoon Rhee play "king of the mountain" in Palos Verdes, California in 1969.

Bruce Lee and Jhoon Rhee watch Otis Hooper, a Jhoon Rhee student, breaking a board during a demonstration given at the University of Maryland in 1968.

Bruce Lee presents a trophy to one of the Jhoon Rhee National Championship winners in 1967.

Jhoon Rhee's favorite portrait of Bruce Lee, from the Jhoon Rhee Collection.

Brandon Lee at a visit to the Rhees in 1968.

Shannon Lee, actress in the television series "Martial Law," with Jhoon Rhee at the annual meeting of the Bruce Lee Educational Foundation in Las Vegas, April 2000.

112

Jhoon Rhee teaches Muhammad Ali a taekwondo sidekick, in preparation for Ali's match against Antonio Inoki in Tokyo on June 27, 1976.

Jhoon Rhee in Hong Kong with Bruce Lee's friends and students. Herb Jackson (second from left), and Ted Wong (far right).

114

Bruce Lee and Jhoon Rhee on stage at the 1967
Jhoon Rhee National Championships in the
National Guard Armory in Washington, D.C.

Chapter Ten

Bruce Predicts
Fame and Fortune

*"I, Bruce Lee, will be the highest
paid Oriental superstar in
the United States. In return I will
give the most exciting performances
and render the best of quality
in the capacity of an actor.*
—Bruce Lee

Although Bruce was disappointed that "The Silent Flute" was stalled, he started getting more and more offers from producers. His first real acting part since his Kato days came in the opening episode of the 1970 television series "Longstreet," which starred James Franciscus as a blind detective. Bruce worked with Stirling Silliphant on the story, and played an antique dealer who becomes the detective's teacher and mentor. Silliphant entitled this episode "The Way of the Intercepting Fist," which is the literal translation of Bruce's style, jeet kune do. "We had more fan mail on that episode than any other in the series," Silliphant has recalled, and has said he thinks the "Longstreet" episode was Bruce's first good film.[20]   On that first "Longstreet" episode, Bruce was depicted as a perfect teacher, and the mystic simplicity of his lessons really came through. I remember watching the show and being impressed with both the storyline and Bruce's acting.

After the excellent reviews of Bruce's acting came out in papers across the country, he wrote a short note to himself, "My Definite Chief Aim":

> "I, Bruce Lee, will be the highest paid Oriental superstar in the United States. In return I will give the most exciting performances and render the best of quality in the capacity of an actor. Starting in 1970, I will achieve world fame and from then onward till the end of 1980, I will have in my possession $10,000,000. Then I will live the way I please and achieve inner harmony and happiness."[21]

116

I was there in the room when Bruce wrote that note; we were at the Los Angeles home of a mutual martial artist friend. I can say with absolute assurance that he was very serious about this goal and promise. Bruce often made such predictions, for one reason, to motivate himself. I have no doubt that, if he'd lived, he would have made the $10 million and become the highest-paid Asian-American superstar.

Shortly before the filming of the "Longstreet" episode, Bruce had made a short trip to Hong Kong, where he found to his complete surprise that he was regarded as a major star. "The Green Hornet"

[21]Lee, p. 96.

had been shown on television throughout Asia, and had galvanized public opinion about Hong Kong's native son. Even the films Bruce had made as a child star had been resurrected, and were popular all over again. He gave demonstrations on live TV, and the viewing audiences were glued to their seats as Bruce performed.

The fact that Bruce was already well-known and widely admired in his native city wasn't lost on him: "After I left Hong Kong the media there kept in touch with me by telephone. Those guys used to call me early in the morning and kept the conversation going on the air so the public was listening to me. Then one day, the announcer asked me if I would do a movie there. When I replied that I would do it if the price was right, I began to get calls from producers in Hong Kong and Taiwan. The offers varied from $2000 to $10,000."[22] Bruce wasn't quite ready to commit to the conditions the Hong Kong studios demanded of their actors—long hours under less than Hollywood conditions, to say the least. But before he was able to negotiate from his position of relative strength, his life took another turn, one that saddened me greatly.

117

One morning in 1970, Bruce began his morning workout as he usually did, with his "Good Morning" exercise, which involved putting a heavy weight across his shoulders, then bending from the waist and straightening up repeatedly. I, too, have my daily rituals—a total fitness program I've developed over five decades

---

[22]Ibid., from an interview in *Fighting Stars* magazine

that I call *RheeShape,:The Balanced Life Program*—and Bruce and I often talked about how important our conditioning regimens were, both to our artistry and our lives. But on this particular morning, either because he had loaded too much weight on the barbell, or because he hadn't warmed up properly, Bruce felt a twinge in his lower back. He ignored it and continued with his workout. Over the next few days, the pain in his back gradually worsened, until it was severe enough to send him to one doctor, then several more. The diagnosis was serious: He had damaged his fourth sacral nerve, in the lumbar region of his spine, and the damage was permanent. The prescription was indefinite bed rest. The doctors told Bruce that he would never be able to practice martial arts again, that his condition would prevent him from kicking with either leg for the rest of his life.

118

This was, of course, devastating news. Bruce was forced into a period of frustrating inactivity that was aggravated by financial troubles and worries about supporting his young family. Eventually, Linda found a job working for an answering service, leaving Bruce home to look after the children (Brandon was five, and in kindergarten, and Shannon was less than a year old). As a traditional Chinese man, Bruce found this situation humiliating, and the Lees did their best to hide their problems from their friends.

Although he was very depressed, Bruce decided to use the time to research and write extensively about kung-fu and jeet kune do, drawing on his ever-expanding library of books about the martial arts of the world. He worked partly to keep his spirits up—to try to use the power of positive thinking to heal his injury—and partly to try to clarify his own thinking about the martial arts and the philosophy he had developed over time. In the end, Bruce decided not to publish, worried that he would discourage his readers from finding their own path in the martial arts. Linda would eventually edit his notes, and publish them posthumously as *The Tao of Jeet Kune Do*. I'm so glad she published the book. It is an invaluable contribution to the canon of martial arts books and to our understanding of Bruce Lee.

After six months, Bruce couldn't endure his enforced inactivity any longer. He decided to begin a moderate round of workouts, and to resume teaching. Over time, he "willed" himself to resume more and more of his old routines—despite the doctors' initially gloomy prognoses—until he began to regain the strength and agility he had before his injury. Still, his back caused him chronic pain for the rest of his life.

119

Chapter Eleven

Bruce the Prolific Writer; Letters Eleven Through Sixteen

"He soared through the air, catapulting his foot through the boards and launching one high above everyone's head and through a brightly lit TV light, smashing it into hundreds of pieces"
—Jhoon Rhee

Letter Eleven

This letter was written in the spring of 1970, and it demonstrates Bruce's efforts in helping me place advertisements in *Black Belt* magazine for the upcoming summer camp for my taekwondo students and practitioners of all other martial arts. I was not aware that advertising space for that publication must be reserved at least three months in advance. Oh well. I still received a good number of applications from enrollees and ended up conducting a successful camp.

Also at that time, I was looking for a few more taekwondo instructors for my growing number of martial arts schools. We

Letter Eleven

Jhoon,

First of all, it's too late to put your training camp once more into B.B. The magazine is already out to the press. I would say about 10 days too late....

Anyway, I called Wu Ngan in England. He does know some basic of martial art and I've told him to watch and practice by himself. He will visit more dojos around the areas.

Enclosed you will find the return sheets and I hope you will submit it in at your earliest convenience and do keep me up to date on it.

Take Care and have fun
(P.S. but not too much fun as the sauna is not here yet)—threaten the man with kicks, punches, strangulations, etc. etc.

Bruce

122

Jhoon,

First of all, it's too late to put your training camp once more into B.B. The magazine is already out to the press, I would say about 18 days too late -----

Anyway, I called Wu Ngan in England. He does know some basic of martial art and I've told him to watch and practice by himself. He will visit more dojos around his areas.

Enclosed you will find the return sheets and I hope you will submit it in as your earliest convenience and do keep me up to date on it were operating eight Jhoon Rhee Schools then, but my goal was to open at least 30 schools in the Washington, D.C. metropolitan area and 1,000 schools nationwide. As the main telephone number for my business, I obtained 202-USA-1000, to illustrate this goal and also because it was easy to remember. Anyway, one of Bruce's students from Hong Kong was living in England. Wu Ngan's wish was to come to teach martial arts in America. He sounded like he'd be perfect for my schools. I sponsored him to come to America but because of strict U.S. immigration policy, he had to wait more time than he wanted. So, he had time to practice by himself in England until his visa was issued. I asked him to find one of the taekwondo schools in London, so he would be ready for teaching as soon as he arrived in Washington.

Bruce eventually would travel to Hong Kong, where he'd achieve big success (which I'll describe below), and decided to bring Wu Ngan to Hong Kong to live in his house. So, Wu never came to America.

Letter Twelve

In this correspondence, Bruce is writing his first letter with the IBM typewriter I had given him. I knew he'd learn to use it and hoped it would encourage his writing. Although Bruce discusses a movie project in this correspondence, I'd rather discuss something he mentions at the bottom of the letter. He writes that he would try to get me publicity for my schools on TV if he were to go on a publicity tour. It never materialized but once again, Bruce shows his generosity.

He also demonstrates some of his infectious optimism when he writes about the importance of aiming high to achieve one's goals. From the numerous conversations and letter exchanges we'd shared, Bruce knew that I had lofty goals—one of which was my aim to have 1,000 schools—and here he was encouraging me to accomplish as much as I wanted because I "have what it takes," as he put it. He had acted as an intermediary with *Black Belt* for an article the magazine was running about my schools, and he made sure to speak highly of my operations, including the "decorations" of my school.

124

Bruce was right, if I may say so myself: My taekwondo facility was of the highest quality. I had 5,000 square feet of studio space for my school, which I rented for the exorbitant price (for those days) of $3,000 a month. It was very luxurious with a top-of-the-line sauna, and I know that Bruce was impressed with it. In fact, he told Kareem Abdul-Jabbar, the basketball star who was also Bruce's student, all about my facility. One day out of the blue, Jabbar walked into my studio, and I was happily surprised. He said, "Bruce Lee told me to visit you." I liked Jabbar, but he was too tall for me to spend too much time walking around with him. I looked like a midget next to him! And my neck would get stiff from constantly looking up.

The purpose of this letter is twofold: First, to show off the typewriter; second, to keep you up on the latest here in the West.

We had a meeting on Project "Leng" last Friday, Coburn, Stirling, and I. Project "Leng" is a code name for our martial art motion picture. Leng is a Chinese word meaning beautiful. Anyway, there is a big breakthrough. Stirling didn't mind his nephew Mark being taken off the writing job, and him and Coburn are both in to hire a professional to do the job. We will speed up the process as soon as the writer comes up with the treatment. We will have another meeting this coming week. Everything is going big gun. Also, Stirling is preparing another film, and he wants me to be his associate producer and technical advisor for the picture—a Japanese sumarai picture. Coburn might be in it too. It will be three months work in Japan. If things go smoothly, the picture can start in six months, then after that, our picture, project "Leng" beautiful, beautiful indeed.

I might go on that publicity tour for MGM yet, though they are not too happy with the money I asked. We will see. If I should go, I will get you on with me for publicity for your school, especially on National T.V.

Remember my friend, everything goes to those who aim to get. Low aim is the biggest crime a man has. One will never get any more than he thinks he can get. You have what it takes. Look back and see your progress—damn the torpedo, full speed ahead!

By the way, Black Belt called and asked me for additional information on your 道場

You can rest assured that what I filled in had to make your school the greatest dojo there is. The fact that you are the most generous furnisher of decorations, 'around' three thousand dollars rent, ect., ect., I can't even remember what I told the secretary.

Delgado opened a school here. He will compete in Parker's tournament next

The purpose of this letter is twofold: First, to show off the typewriter; second, to keep you up on the latest here in the West.

week, so is Joe Lewis. Lewis latest wish is to become a professional boxer.

Well my friend, take good care and my best regards to Han Soon and the family. By the way, how is little 'abagee'?

Bruce

125

Bruce ends the letter with his usual warmth. When he mentions "abagee," he's referring to my second daughter who was a toddler at the time. Just for the record, the term actually means "father" in Korean. Bruce had it mixed up but, out of politeness, he certainly tried to learn a little of my language. And, he often did use Korean expressions correctly.

Letters Thirteen, Fourteen & Fifteen

In the May 28th letter, Bruce is following up on his recommendation of Wu Ngan. He's also expressing some renewed hope that "The Silent Flute" will be produced with James Coburn as one of its stars. As you can see from each of these letters, Bruce has loaded up his schedule for the next few months with lots of travel. He will fly to New York and then come to my tournament in Washington. He plans to fly to Rome in August and, before that, he will go with me to a special tournament of mine in the Dominican Republic. I'll get into that in the next section.

Letter Sixteen

Bruce wrote his next letter to me in the early summer of 1970. He had just attended my annual championships and I was probably still laughing when I received this short note. You see, Bruce and Linda pulled off another funny skit and, from a strictly entertainment perspective, it was one of the most engaging

Mr. Jhoon Goo Rhee
2000 L Street N.W.
Washington D.C. 20001

May 27, 1970

Dear Jhoon Rhee,

From a recent issue of Black Belt Magazine I have noticed your want ad for assistant instructors. From my past association with you, I know you just might be interested in the skill of a Chinese friend of mine by the name of Wu Ngan. Mr. Wu is originally from my home town Hong Kong, and is currently residing in London. Should you like to pursue this matter further, you can reach me by phone to my home just about any hour in the evening. (Tel: 472-1904) I will give you more background and information regarding Mr. Wu.

Sincerely yours,

Bruce

Mr. Jhoon Goo Rhee
2000 L Street N.W.
Washinton D.C. 20001

Dear Jhoon Rhee,   May 27 1970

From a recent issue of Black Belt Magazine I have noticed your want ad for assistant instructors. From my past association with you, I know you just might be interested in the skill of a Chinese friend of mine by the name of Wu Ngan. Mr. Wu is originally from my home town Hong Kong, and is currently residing in London. Should you like to pursue this matter further, you can reach me by phone to my home just about any hour in the evening. (Tel:472-1904) I will give you more background and informations regarding Mr. Wu.

Sincerely yours,

Bruce Lee

Letter Thirteen

127

Letter Fourteen

Dear Jhoon Goo,   May 28, 1970

By now you should have received the letter I wrote for the recommendation of 全 仔. Enclosed find Gung Fu 5th rank certificate. In your next letter do explain in detail what will actually take place.

We have just finished our final script meeting and next week Stirling will come once more to Wash. D.C. and I'm sure he will contact you by phone, maybe coming down to your gym and workout.

Jim Coburn also will leave for Europe for his film and "Silent Flute" will become his next picture hopefully as soon as he completes this one. I'll meet him in Rome this coming August.

Talking about trip, see what date in July you plan for the Dominican Republic trip, I think the middle of July will be fine. In August I have quite a few cities to covered in Europe.

Am training very hard now to get into the best shape for the coming film, spending every day on self-improvement.

Well, take care my friend and do let me know the procedure for getting Wu Ngan over from England.

Bruce

128

may 28 1970

Dear Jhoon Goo,
By now you should have received the letter I wrote for the recomendation of 全 仔. Enclosed find Gung Fu 5th rank certificate. In your next letter do explain in detail what will actually take place.
We have just finished our final script meeting and next week stirling will come once more to Wash. D.C. and I'm sure he will contact you by phone, maybe coming down to your gym and workout.
Jim Coburn also will leave for Europe for his film and "silent Flute" will become his next picture hopefully as soon as he completes this one. I'll meet him in Rome this coming August.

Dear Jhoon Rhee,

I have just made arrangements with my agent. I believe I will come to your tournament. If in the event that something do come up, my agent will contact me wherever I happen to be at the moment.

However, there is a slight change of flight plan—that is, the Eastern Airline ticket for my guest from New York to Wash. D.C. will be cancelled. Instead, make arrangement so that I will fly from New York to Seattle, to Oakland, then back to Los Angeles. In other word, the flight arrangements for the trip will be Los Angeles to New York to Wash. D.C. to New York to Seattle to Oakland to Los Angeles. I'll discard the previous tickets you sent and wait for the revised one. Leave the date of flight open as I have to schedule my time. Of course, only one hotel room is required during my stay in Wash. And I will try to come up Friday instead.

In your return letter let me know the name of hotel that I'm staying in Wash. Plus your phone number, both home and gym in case that something comes up.

See you soon.
Bruce Lee

Letter Fifteen

129

demonstrations I had ever seen from Bruce. He acted like a street bum and Linda acted as a young lady dressed in an elegant evening gown. The bum was making fun of the beautiful lady and bothering her with nasty looks and rude language. They carried on like this for awhile—just long enough to tease the crowd and make them wonder where the skit was going. But soon the lady could no longer ignore her pest. Linda suddenly punched, kicked and threw her husband over her shoulder and onto the floor. Bruce pretended to be out cold, as he lay flat on his back, and was carried off the stage. The audience burst into laughter and applause, just as they had a few years earlier when Bruce and Linda performed the gag I described in a previous passage.

When he wrote this letter, the contract to publish my book series was signed, sealed and delivered, and, it was only a matter of time before Mito Uyehara at *Black Belt* published and printed the English version of my books. Bruce was really looking forward to seeing and reading them. Without his influence on Mito, I doubt they would have been published.

He ended the note with a mention of our late July 1970 get-together, a visit in Washington at my house before a trip to one of my tournaments in the Dominican Republic. Considering how busy he was with other business and how much pain his back was causing him, it was especially gracious of Bruce to come to the Dominican Republic to perform a demo to help boost

Dear Jhoon Rhee,

Finally arrived L.A. to-day (July 2) but early to-morrow morning I have to start another long journey again to New York first and then Mass.

It was indeed nice to have gotten together with you in New York; that one brief stay in Wash. D.C. was most enjoyable.

Will be looking forward for the English version of the Tae Kwon Do book.

See you around July 30.

Bruce Lee

Letter Sixteen

131

enrollment at the event. And, what a demo that turned out to be, despite his obvious physical pain. I was reminded of it several years ago when the basketball superstar Michael Jordan, suffering with a severe case of the flu, played one of his most spectacular playoff games ever. Sometimes the human will can supersede the most adverse conditions—at least when that human will has the fortitude and talent of a Jordan or a Lee.

Before we left the country, Bruce came to visit my wife Han Soon and me for a couple of days. The first day he arrived we did our usual socializing, our own distinct brand of "partying": we went out to restaurants and ate spicy Asian food, talked about martial arts and worked out. Then, at the end of the day Bruce said, "Hey Jhoon, we never do any board-breaking routines. Is it hard?" Bruce expressing an interest in this was unusual because he generally looked down on this element of martial arts. I said, "No, it's not hard. In fact, with your power, you can do it better than most people."

So Bruce did a few kicks through some boards I had lying around my garage—we didn't dare do any of this in my living room, nor would my wife have allowed us to!—and pretty soon he was better than me. During this practice time, he broke three one-inch boards that were just dangling from the rafters. He just jumped as high as he could and side-kicked the boards in half. And, he didn't stop. He practiced the entire following day and into the night, breaking more than 100 boards. At one point, I had to go out to the lumberyard to get more wood. He wanted to come as close to perfecting this new skill as he could, so that he could perform it in the Dominican Republic. When we got there, reporters from the local TV station had come to the tournament, in large part to film Bruce's demo. Bruce dazzled the crowd with his usual repertoire, and then he had an assistant bring out some boards. Bruce took a few steps back, focused in on his target and took off for a flying jump-kick. He soared through the air, catapulting his foot through the boards and launching one high above everyone's head and through a brightly lit TV light, smashing it into hundreds of pieces. It was spellbinding! The tournament crowd went nuts!

What's more, he didn't complain about his back the entire trip. I'm sure it was hurting, but maybe he was beginning to come to grips mentally with the pain, at least that's what I was hoping on the flight back to the States. His new board-breaking skill gave him an emotional lift. And clearly, it gave all who saw it—either live or later on television—an even deeper appreciation for Bruce Lee.

133

Chapter Twelve

Offers Roll In From Hong Kong; and Letter Seventeen

" You have a tendency to waste a lot of your energy in worry and anticipation. Remember my friend to enjoy your planning as well as your accomplishment, for life is too short for negative energy "
—Bruce Lee

In spite of the many setbacks and disappointments Bruce had endured while he tried to break into the movie business, he remained focused on Hollywood and the United States as his route to fame. Though he was aware of his growing popularity in Hong Kong and elsewhere in Asia because of the syndication of "The Green Hornet," Bruce knew from his childhood experiences that the Hong Kong studio system was even more fickle and paternalistic than its American counterpart. But in late summer 1970, before his debut episode of "Longstreet" had made it to American TV screens, Bruce began receiving increasingly more film offers from the heads of the Hong Kong studios.

The first offer came from Run Run Shaw, a former refugee from Shanghai who had helped establish the Hong Kong film industry. Shaw Brothers had a near-monopoly on movie-making in the colony, as well as a chain of successful movie theaters across Southeast Asia. Bruce heard through friends in the business in Hong Kong that an offer was on the way from Run Run Shaw—but when it arrived, he found it hard to take seriously. Shaw offered a paltry $2,000 a film, and expected Bruce to sign a multi-picture deal. Bruce eventually asked some questions about the scripting and casting of Shaw's film. Shaw's response was curt and offended Bruce, so he cut off negotiations with Shaw. This is typical of Bruce, as he treated people with respect and expected the same in return. As it happened, another offer was waiting in the wings.

Raymond Chow had been a producer for Run Run Shaw for years, but had quit in early 1970 to start his own studio, Golden Harvest. It was a big gamble for Chow to take on the Shaw Brothers' monopoly. His initial financing allowed Chow to make a few low-budget (even by Hong Kong standards) pictures, that made modest profits, keeping the studio afloat. But the Shaw Brothers controlled distribution throughout much of Asia, and could deny Chow's movies the venues they needed to be seen at all. Golden Harvest struggled from the beginning. There were bitter feelings between Run Run Shaw and Raymond Chow, and their feud only intensified when Chow made a bid for Bruce to star in his upcoming action picture, "The Big Boss." Bruce always had his ear to the ground about the personalities and politics on matters that concerned him so he knew much about the inner workings and maneuverings of the Hong Kong film establishment. That's just the way he was: curious, clever and savvy.

But my friend's admirer, Chow, also made it a point to learn about Bruce and what made him tick. So he approached Bruce more carefully than did Shaw. He sent a senior producer as an emissary to Los Angeles to negotiate. The producer, Liu Liang Hwa, was the wife of Lo Wei, one of Chow's directors; Bruce was to have a complex and rocky relationship with Lo Wei as events unfolded (ultimately ending up in mutual death threats, as I understand it), but at the time he knew only that Chow was making a serious offer. The whole time that Bruce spent in discussions with Chow's representative, he was receiving phone calls and telegrams from rival producers. The calls and messages continued long after Bruce signed the contract, and even when he was on location in rural Thailand. One producer from Taiwan got through to Bruce, and "[t]he guy told me to rip up the contract, and he'd top Raymond's offer and even take care of any lawsuit for breaking the agreement," Bruce said. [23]

137

Bruce eventually signed on with Golden Harvest for two films, at $7,500 per film. At the time, this was considered real money for an actor in Hong Kong. He once expressed to me his high hopes about the movie contracts in a way that suggested some-

---

[23]Lee, p. 100.

thing like this: "Phew, it's about time!" Still, he had no illusions about the kind of movies he would be making. While he negotiated the deal, Bruce watched some of the most recent Shaw and Chow productions.

"They were awful. For one thing, everybody fights all the time, and what really bothered me was that they all fought exactly the same way. Wow, nobody's really like that. When you get into a fight, everybody reacts differently, and it is possible to act and fight at the same time. Most Chinese films have been very superficial and one-dimensional."[24]

But Bruce told me he needed to make an entry into the film market, keep his name in the public's eye and continue to get exposure to producers and directors so that one day he could make complex, creative and intelligent films. (He also needed the money.) I believe he was smart to think this way and offered him whatever encouragement I could.

Letter Seventeen

Bruce's deep philosophical leanings are apparent in many of the letters he sent to me, for example in Letter Three with the poem "Who Am I and Which Are You?" He wrote his next letter in the spring of 1971, a time of transition for him. He was coming to grips with two realizations: "The Silent Flute," would not be res-

---

[24]Lee, p. 100.

urrected; and, his back—while certainly healing more than the doctors initially had predicted—would plague him for the rest of his life. He had needed to cancel a few of his private lessons and curtail much of his physical activity. Yet, on the other hand, as I described in the above section, his acting career was back on track in Hong Kong and his back had shown real improvement over the last few weeks. I do maintain that he jumped a psychological hurdle regarding his back with his brave and sensational performance in the Dominican Republic.

Incidentally, "The Silent Flute" was made after Bruce's death. Retitled "Circle of Iron" and released in 1978, it starred David Carradine in the multiple roles originally written for Bruce. Despite Carradine's stardom from the hit TV series "Kung Fu," the film was a critical and box-office disappointment.

At this intriguing juncture of his life, Bruce was reading, or in many cases, re-reading his collection of books on the philosophy of positive thinking. He loved the motivational works of Napoleon Hill, Paul Myer, Norman Vincent Peale, and many others. We shared this philosophical outlook—both regarding the martial arts and life in general. One paragraph of the letter really stands out. I'm repeating it here because it shows Bruce's intellectual maturity for such a young man and because I find these words very profound and inspirational:

Letter Seventeen

140

Jhoon Goo,

Greetings from Los Angeles where, like every place in the states, business is not too good. Don't misunderstand me that this is a pessimistic statement. Though the fact is just as it is, but like anybody else, you have your choice of reacting to it. Here I ask you Jhoon Goo, are you going to make your obstacles stepping stones to your dream, or stumbling blocks because unknowingly you let negativeness, worries, fear, etc. to take over you?

Believe me that in every big thing or achievement there is always obstacles, big or small, and the reaction one shows to such obstacles is what counts, not the obstacle itself. There is no such thing as defeat until you admit so yourself, but not until then!

My friend do think of the past in terms of those memories of events and accomplishments which were pleasant, rewarding and satisfying. The present? Well, think of it in terms of challenges and opportunities, and the rewards available for the application of your talents and energies. As for the future, that is a time and a place where every worth ambition you possess is within your grasp.

You have a tendency to waste a lot of your energy in worry and anticipation. Remember my friend to enjoy your planning as well as your accomplishment, for life is too short for negative energy.

Since the Indian trip my back is so so. "Silent Flute" is still on with Warner Bro. We are waiting to hear the next step, and should know within ten days—approval of new budget, setting up another survey trip, etc. Aside from "Silent Flute," I will do a guest appearance on a new T.V. series "Longstreet" for next season. Then there is another movie that I will do (one of the three leading character) should the presentation be approved, and that we should know within ten days or so too.

So remember that one who is possessed by worry not only lack the poise to solve his own problems, but by his nervousness and irritability creates additional problem for those around him.

Of course the damn thing is I want to do something now! So I have created a T.V. series idea and I should know within a couple of weeks. In the meantime I am working on another idea for a movie to do in Hong Kong (Chinese Movie).

So action! Action! Never wasting energy on worries and negative thoughts. I mean who has the most insecure job as I have

What do I live on? My faith in my ability that I'll make it. Sure my back screwed me up good for a year but with every adversity comes a blessing because a shock acts as a reminder to oneself that we must not get stale in routine. Look at a rain storm. After its departure, everything grows!

So remember that one who is possessed by worry not only lacks the poise to solve his own problems, but by his nervousness and irritability creates additional problems for those around him.

Well, what more can I say but damn the torpedo, full speed ahead!!

From a martial artist
with a screwed up
back but who has discovered
a new powerful kick!

Bruce Lee's middle name in Chinese characters means "little" and his last name means "dragon." In this letter to Jhoon Rhee, he playfully wrote the Chinese character for "big" rather than for "little". Here Jhoon Rhee has written Bruce Lee's actual middle name in Chinese characters.

His Real name is 李小龍 (小) means small
                        → mean Dragon

He wrote   李大龍 (大) means big or large

(He is playing with me that he is not small dragon
                                    but a large dragon

My friend, do think of the past in terms of those memories of events and accomplishments which were pleasant, rewarding and satisfying. The present? Well, think of it in terms of challenges and opportunities, and the rewards available for the application of your talents and energies. As for the future, that is a time and a place where every worthy ambition you possess is within your grasp.

It's important to explain that in his letter Bruce was projecting, as the psychologists say, many of his feelings onto me. He was generalizing for all of us, really. I often wonder if Bruce would have succeeded in academia as a philosophy professor. I think he could have done very well in front of a college class. Some of his pontificating was quite instructional, shamanistic almost.

142

Interestingly, Bruce and I were simultaneously dealing with the same philosophical theme which he elucidated in this letter. Let me explain. At about this time, I had developed our beginner's sparring training program called "Double Counter." This drill is for students to develop a habit of counterattacking a second, a third or even a fourth time until their final counterattack is a success. Persistence is the key because, as Bruce pointed out, there are "always obstacles." Think of examples from your own life. Let's say you opened your own martial arts studio or a restaurant and, for one reason or another, you had to close the business after six months. Now, you know your concept is good but maybe your business plan is not sound. Would you be discouraged and quit the business for good, or try again using your past experience as a "stepping stone" (another of Bruce's favorite expressions) for success?

In order to reach your worthy goal, you may have to fall a few times first, no matter what that goal may be. Will you stay in your fallen position or stand up, again and again, until you reach your goal? If you stay in your fallen position, you are permanently defeated. You are not defeated, however, so long as you are standing up and trying again—"damn the torpedo, full speed ahead!!" This is what Bruce was telling me, but more importantly, telling himself in this letter.

Even though he acknowledges his "screwed up back," as he closed the letter, he also mentioned his "new powerful kick." He's referring to a sliding-skip side kick that I had recently shown him. Bruce was able to generate so much forceful and fast momentum that his version of this kick became stronger than mine after he practiced it only a few times!

143

Chapter Thirteen

Bruce Becomes a "Big Boss"

"That is Mr. Jhoon Rhee's Accupunch. It moves at tremendous speed with no warning and accelerates like a bullet in flight. You can hardly see it."
—Muhammad Ali

In July 1971, a few months after Bruce wrote the previous letter, he flew to Hong Kong to begin work on the movie "The Big Boss." Because there was the continuing threat of further intrigue from the Shaw Brothers and others, Raymond Chow decided to whisk Bruce as directly as possible to the remote village in Thailand where the film would be shot. Bruce spent only a short time between flights in the Hong Kong airport, meeting up with a friend, then caught a connecting flight to Bangkok. When he arrived in the damp heat of July in Pak Chong, he met Raymond Chow for the first time. The two shook hands, and Lee told Chow: "You just wait, I'm going to be the biggest Chinese star in the world."[25] Then both men laughed.

[25]Lee, p. 101.

That's the way Bruce would approach most things he'd do—with confidence (that some called cockiness) but also with a sense of humor, as if to assure everyone that his strong self-esteem was in check.

Rural Thailand in July of 1971 was a miserable place to be, but Bruce tried to make the best of it, ignoring the hardships—the bad food, yellow tap water, nonexistent sanitation and mosquitoes—as well as the low production values of Chow's studio. He was making a movie at last, and he was determined to get the very most out of this opportunity.

But powerful obstacles stood in the way. The first director was renowned for his uncontrollable temper. For the first five days of filming, he abused the cast and crew at the top of his lungs until the production manager, the same Liu Liang Hwa who had been dispatched to Los Angeles to negotiate with Bruce, had had enough. She called Raymond Chow from Bangkok, and convinced him to fire the director and hire as a replacement Lo Wei, who was, perhaps not so coincidentally, her husband. Bruce observed all this with as much detachment as he could muster. In letters to Linda by way of the unreliable Thai postal service, he describes his situation:

"Another director (a fame lover) just arrived, supposedly to take over the present director's job. It really doesn't matter as long as he is capable as well as cooperative...The food is terrible, this village has no beef and very little chicken and pork...I wish you were here because I miss you and the children a lot. This village is terrible. No place like home..."[26] Bruce truly felt that way, I'm sure, as he often lamented having to travel and spend time away from his family. And, I'd like to think, he probably wished he could've eaten a few platefuls of my wife's cooking that he loved so much.

And again, on July 28, he wrote: "The film I'm doing is quite amateur-like. A new director has replaced the uncertain old one; this new director [Lo Wei] is another so-so one with an almost unbearable air of superiority. At any rate, I'm looking forward to leaving Pak Chong for Bangkok where it is at least halfway decent...It's been 15 days since my arrival in Pak Chong and already it seems like a year! Due to lack of meat, I have to get canned meat for lunch. I'm glad to have brought along my vitamins..."[27] Here we see that Bruce had the foresight to have packed his vitamins, which he took daily—without fail. These days, it seems everyone takes vitamins but back then not many people did. In this regard, as in others, Bruce was ahead of his time.

147

In a later interview, Bruce described one of the other aspects of filming in a tiny Third World village: "We used all existing

[26]Lee, p. 102.
[27]Lee, p. 103.

locations. Even the whorehouse was real and it was very dirty and it stunk. And the poor prostitutes were very ugly. They got 15 patts a trick, which is about 75 cents, and the production company paid them 200 patts not to do anything and keep out of the way."[28] By the way, Bruce told me that he would never actually go to a brothel, that he was only told about the conditions inside the houses of prostitution and didn't doubt what he had heard.

Eventually, after several hectic weeks of filming, during which he cut his hand severely enough to require ten stitches, and twisted his ankle, Bruce made it back to Bangkok. Here, he exulted in ordering breakfast in bed in his air-conditioned hotel. He talked about his future acting career at this point with a new confidence and assurance; while he had been "lost" in remote back country Thailand, the season-opening episode of "Longstreet" had run on American network TV, and the universally favorable notices were the catalyst for a mad scramble by Paramount to locate Bruce. This, in turn, raised his value in the eyes of the filmmakers in Hong Kong. "They [Paramount] couldn't get me because I really was in the sticks. It's funny, but when Paramount sent telegrams and telephoned Hong Kong for me, boy, the producers there thought I was an important star. My prestige must have increased threefold."[29]

When Paramount did get a hold of Bruce, they offered him $1,000 per episode to appear in three more "Longstreet" shows.

---

[28]Clouse, p. 98.
[29]Lee, p. 106.

He felt that he was bargaining from strength, with a signed contract for another film with Golden Harvest, so he asked for double the money. Paramount agreed; Bruce was now a hot property. When I learned of his hard-stance bargaining position, I smiled because Bruce Lee, the philosopher, the martial artist, the actor, the funny guy, and all-around good person was now Bruce Lee the shrewd businessman.

But the bad news was: the three "Longstreet" episodes were disappointing, both to Bruce and to the critics. The season premiere had been written by Silliphant as a vehicle for Bruce; his remaining appearances were shoe-horned into existing scripts, and were little more than cameos. It seemed that American television wasn't ready for Bruce Lee after all. By October, 1971, Warner Brothers had made an offer to option Bruce for $25,000 for his own series. The studios now took his box-office potential seriously, but he was undecided about committing himself to television, especially after he received repeated warnings from his friend and pupil James Coburn that television would wear him down in 13 weeks, the length of one television season. Coburn and others advised Bruce to work through Hong Kong, rather than Hollywood. I told Bruce that, as well, because I knew he could make it big in Hong Kong.

Bruce's plan, as far as he had formed one, was to complete his contract with Raymond Chow, and then most likely accept one of the American television offers, returning to resettle his family and work in the United States. He would continue to visualize his career as based in Hollywood even after he and Linda had sold their house in Los Angeles, and his success in Hong Kong was overwhelmingly clear.

But when Bruce and his family returned to Hong Kong in October of 1971 for the premiere of "The Big Boss," it was obvious that something was in the wind. There was an enormous throng waiting at Kai Tak Airport, including a Boy Scout brass band, dozens of reporters, and homemade banners welcoming the big star home. This was partly orchestrated by Golden Harvest, to build word of mouth for the premiere of the film, but it was also the first big outpouring of a genuine pride the Chinese public, and Asians in general, were to express over the coming months and years. Bruce was seen by ordinary people as a symbol of Chinese ethnic pride, as well as a rags-to-riches success story. He was the hometown boy making good, and a symbol of Chinese power. I would have loved to have been there, to see him being received so enthusiastically because he deserved all the attention—and then some.

When Bruce, Linda, and the executives of Golden Harvest attended the midnight premiere of "The Big Boss," tension filled the air. Bruce acknowledged to me that he was quite nervous that night. How would the notoriously vocal Hong Kong audience react? If they disapproved of a film, Hong Kong audiences had been known to cut the seats with knives. As it turned out, the crowd was unanimous in its roaring, stamping approval. Bruce and his family had to be hustled out of the theater, past cheering fans and the pop of flashbulbs. One American critic wrote: "[This] film is the finest accomplishment of Bruce Lee's career. It is one of the most outstanding examples of sheer animal presence on the celluloid ever produced. I would match it against the best of Clint Eastwood, Steve McQueen or the various James Bonds."[30]

Another reviewer stumbled on the midnight premiere of the film completely by accident. He was amazed by the vehemence of the audience; he had never heard of this guy, my friend Bruce Lee. "When the film ended there was about ten seconds of silence. They didn't know what hit them, and then they started roaring... And [I had the] feeling...: this guy is going to be IT."[31]

"The Big Boss" broke all box-office records in Hong Kong, selling $3.5 million worth of tickets in 19 days (the previous top seller, "The Sound of Music," grossed $2.3 million in nine weeks). It broke records across Asia, and as far afield as Rome, Beirut and Buenos Aires. Needless to say, Bruce and Linda were relieved as they could now finally feel financially secure. I was relieved, too, because as mentally and spiritually strong as Bruce was, his psyche needed a shot in the arm, so to speak.

---

[30]Lee, p. 107.
[31]Clouse, p. 108.

Bruce said later that he had been confident all along that the film would be a hit, but even he had to admit that he was unprepared for the excitement "The Big Boss" generated throughout Asia and around the world. He explained the martial arts mania that followed the film's release by restating his desire to make films that were about more than just fighting. He wanted there to be many levels to the plot and characters, so that a moviegoer could find more meaning if he looked for it. His character in "The Big Boss" is an ordinary, likable person who finds out that he's been taken advantage of, and then lashes out. This is the beginning of Bruce's transformation of martial arts from a purely "tough guy" image to a more widely accessible part of modern society. This is part of his legacy: the desire to see martial arts as a philosophical pursuit as well as a fighting form. He succeeded and all of us involved in the martial arts benefited from the positive attention Bruce generated.

152

Bruce Lee and Ali

During this time in his life, Bruce became fascinated with Muhammad Ali. He spent hours at the Golden Harvest studio, watching a documentary film of Ali in the ring. He arranged a full-length mirror to reflect Ali as he moved on the screen, then learned the boxer's moves by following them with his own body. "Everybody says I must fight Ali some day," Bruce said. "I'm studying every move he makes. I'm getting to know how he thinks and moves." But he was pessimistic—or should I say realistic—about his chances against the heavyweight champion of the world: "Look at my hand. That's a little Chinese hand. He'd kill me."[32]

Although Bruce never met Muhammad Ali, he did connect with him, posthumously, through me. Let me explain. Bruce taught me an innovative new punch that illustrates his profound philosophy of fighting. He told me that you never telegraph with which hand you will strike. When he demonstrated what he meant by that, he asked me to try and block his punches. As much as I focused, as much as I told myself to quicken my defenses, I couldn't block him. The principle here is that when you decide to punch you are detached. In my own mind, I repositioned the way I thought about this principle. I applied my civil engineering training to fully understand it. Engineers talk about human reaction time. That's the amount of time it takes the brain to tell a body part—in the case of punch-blocking that would be the wrist—to react. Normally, when a fighter sees a punch coming in, his eyes tell the brain: "Brain, tell the wrist to react." That takes time—precious time. The idea is to finish the execution before the opponent finishes the brain-to-wrist communication.

153

I coined a name for Bruce's punch—the "Accupunch"—and one day it was my honor to transfer Bruce's skill and legacy to the heavyweight boxing champion of the world! I first met Muhammad Ali in 1975 before his "Thrilla In Manila" championship fight with Joe

---

[32]Clouse, p. 112.

Frazier. A mutual friend and kung-fu student, Harold Norman, introduced us in what best reflects how people who trust one another can work together for mutual advantage. He said, "I'll introduce you to Muhammad Ali if you give me one of your safety equipment distributorships for me to run in Philadelphia. And, I'll ask Ali to endorse the products." I happily agreed, and we soon made plans to go to Deer Lake, Pa., where Ali trained.

154

I was surprised to learn that Ali had heard of me, but not so surprised that he knew and had tremendous respect for Bruce. Ali talked about how quick Bruce was. I told Ali that Bruce had great respect for him too and that to honor the memory of my friend I would like to show him one of Bruce's most secret weapons. Ali was intrigued and said, "Let's do it!" Later that day, I showed Ali the Accupunch. I punched him and he couldn't block it. People who were watching got a big kick out of this small Korean martial artist getting through Ali's lightning-fast defenses. Then I taught Muhammad Ali the Accupunch just as Bruce had taught me. Subsequently, I was Ali's coach, when he competed in a rare boxing-versus-wrestling match in Japan, and we became friends.

Ali used the Accupunch in his fight against Frazier in Manila, and then he Accupunched the British champ Richard Dunn for a knockout blow. When a reporter was showing Ali a slow-motion replay of his knockout punch, he explained on national TV, "That is Mr. Jhoon Rhee's Accupunch."

However, Ali didn't want to reveal any details of the punch publicly at that time, for his competitors to hear. But at a later time he explained, "I learned the Accupunch from Mr. Jhoon Rhee. It acts at the exact moment you decide to hit, and there is no lag time at all. It is instantaneous. It moves at tremendous speed with no warning and accelerates like a bullet in flight. You can hardly see it."

After the wrestling match in Japan, I asked Ali to go to South Korea with me to meet the people and to allow the most popular man in the world, at the time, the opportunity to give taekwondo some great PR. Over one-million people showed up in June 1976 to cheer for Ali in an open-car parade that hadn't been seen in the country since the people lined the streets for Dwight Eisenhower, after the Korean War. Even though I think of Ali as the original trash talker, he is a very quiet man when he's among close friends—he's also very smart, by the way—but when the media show up, he lights up.

155

Bruce Exhibits His Philosophical Depth Through the Art of Acting

Run Run Shaw and other Hong Kong producers had never given up the idea of luring Bruce away from Raymond Chow and Golden Harvest. Now that his box-office potential was obvious, Shaw and the others redoubled their efforts. Shaw sent a signed contract for $250,000 to Bruce, which Bruce sent back. Shaw then sent a blank check to Bruce, but it was useless: production had already begun on "Fist of Fury," that would become Bruce's next big cinematic hit.

Although Bruce had always taken acting very seriously—he once told me that an actor must have as much mental discipline and steadfast concentration as does a martial artist—he seemed to explore the craft even further as his Hong Kong-based movie career skyrocketed. Bruce also mentioned other qualities an actor must possess. Again, these attributes are similar to those that make a good martial artist: dedication, hard work, and the drive to self-understanding. The actor (as well as the martial artist) must prepare himself in the art of self-expression—prepare physically, psychologically and spiritually, fully realizing that in this lifetime there is no end to the training. While I haven't done much acting, I've done enough to know that I agree with Bruce's comparison.

156

Bruce believed that the depth of an actor's self-realization is clearly visible on the screen, and that is his "presence" as an actor. If he is willing to keep expanding himself, to continue growing, he is bound to radiate the power of his internal energy and integrity as a human being. Only by consciously cultivating his power, and honestly assessing himself, can a person excel as a professional. Bruce was very disparaging of the level of professionalism in the Hong Kong studio system. He held himself and those around him to the same very high standard. His commitment to his fans grew as quickly as his fame. He felt responsible for raising peoples' sights, for educating them about the possibilities of both film and the martial arts.

He was also against the use of violence for its own sake in martial arts films. He preferred the term "action films," by which he meant that fighting in his movies should always serve a purpose. He also maintained that his films should be seen as blending fantasy and reality. They were meant as allegories or fables, rather than street-fighting manuals. The films he made, both as a child and as an adult, were mostly based on popular Chinese myths and legends. He felt that his films were actually far less violent than the standard Hong Kong feature of his time, and far less explicitly gory. I think this is a responsible attitude and wish that we had more action-film stars who felt this way today, more who would shun gratuitous violence, thus shielding our kids from all the blood and guts.

157

Bruce had always been driven to perform whatever he did as perfectly as is humanly possible. "Ever since I was a kid," he once said, "the word quality has meant a great deal to me. The greatest satisfaction is to hear another unbiased human being whose heart has been touched and honestly says, 'Hey, here is someone real!' I'd like that!... No matter what, let your inner light guide you out of darkness."[33]

Unfortunately, with "Fist of Fury," Bruce was once again saddled with Lo Wei. Although Lo was a seasoned director, with more

---

[33]Lee, p. 120.

than 80 action films under his belt, he was as interested in horse racing as in directing films. There were numerous reports of his attention wandering, as he listened to the races, while crucial scenes were being shot. Since the soundtrack was always dubbed in later, Lo could blare his radio at top volume even during quiet love scenes. As if that weren't enough to set off Bruce's temper, the facilities at Golden Harvest's Hong Kong studio were nearly as primitive as those in rural Thailand. And, as often happened in the world of Hong Kong action films, the script was being written more or less at the same time the film was being shot. Bruce chafed at the casual approach Lo took to his art, especially after the overwhelming success of "The Big Boss." The middle-aged Lo, for his part, found Bruce to be arrogant and headstrong, a typical young talent impatient for his turn in the spotlight. Bruce and Lo were bitter antagonists by the time the filming was completed.

Although Bruce and I did not correspond much during these hectic times, I tried to follow what he was doing. I knew that the reception in 1971 for "Fist of Fury" would be at least as frenzied as for "The Big Boss." It was. Even with $2 tickets being scalped for $45, police in Singapore had to ask that "Fist of Fury" be withdrawn for a week, so that they could work out ways to cope with the traffic jams created by the film's opening. The film ran for eight months in the Philippines, and was so popular that the government finally had to order the film withdrawn from theaters for several weeks to allow domestic films to sell some tickets. Once again, Bruce's film broke box-office records in Hong Kong, making $4 million in 13 days. And, once again, the film was a blockbuster worldwide, making Bruce one of the first truly international action stars. My friend's earlier predictions about his fame and fortune were indeed coming true.

June 21, 1972

Dear Bruce:

It has been over half a year since I have seen you. What exciting news to hear that your first movie broke the record of the past one hundred years; and the second movie broke the first one. I always have respected you with your ability and determination, and your positive thinking. I was sure that one way or the other they would come, but I did not think they would come so soon.

159

I have invented a new device for free sparring which is to eliminate injuries for the contestants. The response from the various fighters and instructors has been very exciting, and I am sure these items will revolutionize the martial arts throughout the world. So far I have only a few pairs. As soon as the finalized product comes out I will send the first two pairs to you. I hope I will get the patent soon. I have spent some money to apply the patent in ten different countries.

Please give my warmest regards to your lovely wife, Linda, and the children.

As ever,

Your friend,

Jhoon Rhee

Familiar Plot Hits Home

"Fist of Fury's" storyline was a familiar one to Asian audiences. I had seen in it many familiar elements of plot. In early twentieth century Shanghai, the revered master of a martial arts school dies. At the funeral, members of a rival Japanese martial arts academy insult the dead master. Bruce, believing that the Japanese have poisoned his revered teacher, seeks revenge. He challenges the top Japanese fighter, vanquishing him and an oversized Russian. Just as he reaches his moment of triumph, the hero dies. Bruce once again injected a strong sense of morality into the movie. He didn't want the deadly violence his character demonstrates to be glorified and rewarded so he insisted that "he" die at the end of the film. He didn't have to do this, of course, but he wanted to stay true to his philosophical underpinnings. When I think of this gutsy artistic decision, I am proud once more that he was my friend.

The underlying themes of "Fist of Fury" appealed to the colonized people of Hong Kong, and the rest of Asia: A man is abused and repressed, taking punishment and humiliation with resilience and reserve, and only rising up to triumph over his enemies at the very end. At one point, Bruce's Japanese antagonist in the movie says with a sneer that "China is the sick man of Asia." This insult, which no doubt brought back the Japanese occupation of China in WWII, is only refuted by Bruce's character at the end of the film, after he has dismantled all his opponents: "The Chinese are NOT sick men!" The crowds in Hong Kong reacted enthusiastically to this, to Bruce's strength and the depth of his determination, with righteous howling and frenzies of enthusiasm. Bruce embodied pride, power and, in a sense, a new politics—and many who saw the film recognized this.

One of those was Phil Ochs, the folk singer. Although he had seen the Japanese Samurai movies, Ochs had never seen anything like Bruce before. He first saw Bruce's movies during a five-hour marathon in the Philippines. He was awestruck by the poetry of Bruce's moves (which he compared to that of the ballet master Nureyev, calling it "the science of the body taken to its highest form"). I agree with Och's assessment, which is one reason why I knew Bruce would like my martial arts ballet. He understood and appreciated the fluid movement inherent in each craft—dancing and martial arts.

161

Generally, Bruce's movies involved rival schools of martial artists, in which one school, run by a gentle, peaceful master, is somehow insulted or injured by another. Then, the master's peaceful teachings ("I will teach you to be the best fighters in the world, but you must never use it to harm anyone unless absolutely necessary") are forgotten in the overwhelming thirst for revenge.[34] The star pupil must avenge insults, or more likely murder, by vanquishing masses of fighters, climaxing with the

[34]Lee, p. 116-117.

defeat of the rival school's star fighter(s). And because Bruce held genuine convictions about violence, the hero had to die at the end to pay for his violent excesses.

I think Ochs' evaluation of Bruce and his talent reveals much about Bruce's universal appeal. After all, Ochs was not a martial arts fan before he saw the movie marathon. While he was very impressed with Bruce he was almost equally struck by the audience's boundless enthusiasm for Bruce, the way they yelled and whistled and stamped their feet to cheer Bruce on. By the way, this exuberant reaction was by no means limited to Asian audiences. Western viewers reacted with the same unbridled enthusiasm. One prominent Hollywood director remarked, "Watching a Bruce Lee film in a public movie theater was like attending a live sports event."

Perhaps most importantly, Ochs believed in what he saw—this was no hollow Hollywood spectacle, with camera tricks and breakaway props and stunt doubles and miraculous hidden devices. This was one man using his body in a way that redeemed the use of force by the purity of his motives and the honesty of his intentions (which Ochs saw reflected in the expression on Bruce's face throughout his movies). The determination, concentration and power of Bruce Lee, as much as the force of the blows, is what overwhelms his enemies. That is what

Ochs saw, and he realized that these qualities are what the audience is there to see and cheer. The audience is rooting for the hero, because his motives are sincere, his cause is just, his body is superbly trained, and his physical, psychological and spiritual selves are one self. Bruce was able to simultaneously provide an ethical example and embody a sense of discipline that appealed to people from many walks of life, all over the world; he expanded the idea of what was possible for one person with motivation and a willingness to overcome fear. This is the service he performed for the martial arts. And all of us in the field owe Bruce our gratitude.

Chapter Fourteen

Bruce Rides The Fame Train Yet Still Remembers His Friends

"Bruce had an uncompromising commitment to quality, and because there were some problems with the script, the shooting of the movie["Enter the Dragon"] was repeatedly delayed..."
—Jhoon Rhee

As I've mentioned, Bruce was finally raking in the money, and he was realizing that there were those who might like to take advantage of him. He talked about this with me both before and after he achieved super-celebrity status, and he once told another friend this: "I have money in front of me that is like a mountain. There is so much of it. This money is there if I want to reach out for it. But I must be very, very careful because the people who want me to have this money want to own me. I must be very careful."[35]

While I'm also a little wary of exploitation, I have a different attitude than Bruce and I once expressed my feelings to him. I think every-

[35]Clouse, p. 169.

body is scratching. I'll go ahead and scratch your back but then you scratch mine too. In other words, I don't mind if people make money off me, as long as they don't hurt me. But then again, I can see why Bruce had more concern than I did about this. He was, after all, an international star who was working at breakneck speed.

Letter Eighteen

In November 1972, I received a letter from Bruce, in which he told me that the release of yet another of his films, "The Way of the Dragon," was being delayed by a few weeks. I'm glad he told me, as I was watching the press to see reports on how it was received in Hong Kong.

166

In this correspondence, Bruce wrote that he broached the subject with Raymond Chow about me making a taekwondo film. (You may recall, he earlier called me up and suggested that I get into movie-making.) I was flattered and grateful—not to mention, excited at the prospect of becoming a movie actor, and using yet another venue to expose people to my form of martial arts and my own developing philosophy of life.

"Enter the Dragon"

In 1972, after the release of "The Way of the Dragon," Bruce, driven as ever, moved right into production for his next film, which

Dear Jhoon,

The premier of my new film in Hong Kong has been rescheduled for December 23. Also, I have talked to Mr. Raymond Chow and although a definite idea has not been formed, I think there is this possibility of making a film entitled, Taekwondo. And I think, personally, it will do you a world of good to be the first one to do it and also for public recognition.

I will write again as more developments come about but do notice that the premier night of my film has been rescheduled.

Take Care

Bruce

Letter Eighteen

167

was to be called "Game of Death." There was no script, but when Bruce found out that his friend and protege Kareem Abdul-Jabbar was in Hong Kong on business, he invited the basketball star to stage a fight with him for the movie. The two worked together for a week, and the footage was so good that Bruce decided it would be the climactic last scene of the film. The dramatic sight of Bruce, at five-feet seven inches, fighting a seven-foot, two-inch giant was simply too compelling to bury in the middle of an assortment of other action scenes. As I've mentioned, when Jabbar visited me, I learned what that height disparity feels like.

168

The plot line of the movie, as it began to emerge, revolved around a character, played by Bruce, who searches for a stolen treasure. Eventually, he traces the treasure to a pagoda in Korea. The problem is that each floor is guarded by a deadly martial artist. Bruce must fight his way past his protege Dan Inosanto, master of the Filipino technique of "escrima." Inosanto and Bruce face off with nunchaku, the tethered sticks first introduced to Bruce by Inosanto. After vanquishing Inosanto, Lee had to face Han Jae Chi, a master of Korean hapkido. Knowing Bruce's general distaste for stiff, traditional martial arts, I suspect he got a kick out of disposing of these masters.

The last challenge came from the character played by his friend Jabbar. These three fight sequences were the only parts of "Game of Death" that were filmed with Bruce. The film was eventually released after he died, but the rest of the footage that would be released had to be shot using other actors, making it only marginally a Bruce Lee film.

Bruce stopped working on "Game of Death" after he received an offer from Hollywood that gave him pause. All the time he had been working in Hong Kong, and his movies had been bringing in record profits, he had been pursued by producers with ever-more lucrative offers. The persistent Run Run Shaw continued to send emissaries with blank checks and contracts, but offers came from further and further afield. Even Carlo Ponti, Sophia Loren's husband and producer, made big-money overtures. Bruce was on the crest of the worldwide wave of excitement over kung-fu, and martial arts in general.

169

Although he was realizing his great ambition, becoming the first international Chinese movie star, Bruce recognized the pitfalls of the situation. "It's like I'm in jail," he once said. "I'm like a monkey in the zoo. People looking at me and things like that, and basically I like a simple life and I like to joke a lot. But I cannot speak as freely as before because misinterpretation comes in ... It hasn't changed me ... It's not that I'm proud or better than I ever was, I'm just the same damn old shit."[36]

---

[36]Lee, p. 134-135.

Fred Weintraub, the producer who had worked with Bruce on the development of the "Kung Fu" TV series, had been working behind the scenes to convince Warner Brothers to make a Bruce Lee movie. He had screened "The Big Boss" and "The Way of the Dragon" for Warner executives as each movie had been released, and had gradually brought them around. The fact that Bruce's movies had out grossed "The Godfather" and "The Sound of Music" in many parts of the world had bolstered Weintraub's case. With President Nixon's opening to China in 1972, the thought of the profits to be made from a Chinese-American action movie tipped the balance. In late 1972, Weintraub was able to bring an offer of $500,000 to Hong Kong. Weintraub's production company (with Paul Heller), Sequoia, would become partners with Warner Brothers and Concord to make "Enter the Dragon." If, that is, all the parties could be enticed to make a deal.

170

When Weintraub tried to get Raymond Chow, as one of the partners in Concord, to sign off on the deal, he couldn't seem to get Chow to agree. Chow said the movie would hurt Bruce's career, and laid down conditions that would make Warner Brothers back out. In my dealings with Chow, I learned that he looked out for those he cared about, and he cared a lot about Bruce. I think he only wanted what was best for Bruce. Weintraub was able to get Bruce to agree to the deal, but he had trouble getting Bruce and Chow in one room at the same time because of their hectic schedules. Weintraub tried for two weeks to get the contract signed, and it was only his imminent departure for the United States that got Bruce to pressure Chow into making the deal happen.

Letter Nineteen

With all this activity whirling around Bruce, you'd think he wouldn't have the time or inclination to write to me. But he did. The last letter I ever received from him came in February 1973. In typical Bruce fashion, he was trying to help me and my career. He was reminding me to send to him and Chow a photo of my student who I thought would be good in my film. I had already sent it—three days earlier—but they had not yet received it. (Of course, we didn't have next-day mail service in those days.) Bruce wanted to make sure that I had as much input in the script as I wanted, and encouraged me in this letter to offer "suggestions."

171

As you can see, Bruce was in high spirits. And why not? He had a lucrative new contract on a movie that he was sure would launch his fame even higher, his family was doing well and his back was holding up. He was indeed "excellent." I was doing well, too, except that I had injured my knee during a training session. Bruce showed his typical courteous consideration in mentioning my injury and wishing me well. Although he joked that "a Korean without a good knee is a dead knee," I think he meant to say "dead Korean." He was probably tired from the pressures of his busy life. In the letter I'd sent to Chow that accompanied the photo of my

Letter Nineteen

Mr. Jhoon Rhee   February 9, 1973
2000 L Street N.W.
Washington D.C. 20036
U.S.A.

Dear Jhoon,

I am at Mr. Chow's office at the moment, and both Mr. Chow and I are waiting for the picture of your student that you have promised to send previously.

Mr. Chow has already told his associate to work on the script while I am very busy working in the Warner Brother picture.

So would you please then rush me those photo[s]. So that I can present them to Mr. Chow along with whatever suggestion you would like to make on this possible project together.

I am doing fine—no! I should say excellent. You know how it is. It's so damned good that I cannot bear it. Lots of luck and take care of your knee. A Korean without a good knee is a dead knee.

Warmest personal regards,

Sincerely yours,

Bruce

Mr. Jhoon Rhee   February 9, 1973
2000 L. Street N. W.
Washington D. C. 20036
U. S. A.

Dear Jhoon,

I am at Mr. Chow's office at the moment, and both Mr. Chow and I are waiting for the picture of your student that you have promised to send previously.

Mr. Chow has already told his associate to work on the script while I am very busy working in the Warner Brother picture.

So would you please then rush me those photo. So that I can present them to Mr. Chow along with whatever suggestion you would like to make on this possible project together.

student, I referred to Bruce. "All my students, staff and friends are all excited and happy for me about the taekwondo movie, on the other hand my competitors are not too excited about it," I wrote. "I have confidence that the film will be a big success especially with 'The Little Dragon's' [Bruce's] help." And sure enough, Bruce was a big help in many ways.

Filming Begins, Troubles Ensue

In February 1973, Weintraub's co-producer Paul Heller, the director Robert Clouse, and the American martial artists John Saxon, Jim Kelly and Bob Wall arrived in Hong Kong to begin filming. The whole production took ten weeks, but there were many incidents on and off the set that threatened to derail the entire production. When I heard about all these problems, I worried about Bruce, his career and, mostly, his health.

He was under a great deal of pressure—much of it self-imposed. "Enter the Dragon" was his chance to transform himself from a household word in Hong Kong to a mainstream star in the United States—something that, of course, he wanted badly. This was why he was filmed, for the first time, in both Chinese traditional clothing and tailored western suits. Bruce was certainly dynamic and sometimes he had a short temper, I've been told, although he never got angry with me. Bruce at this time was facing pressure from the Hong Kong press, which seemed to be continually probing for weaknesses in Bruce as a person and as an actor: also, he had to deal with a steady stream of challengers who tried to pick fights with him whenever he appeared in public, and even on the sets of his movies. Bruce had an uncompromising commitment to quality, and because there were some problems with the script, the shooting of the movie was repeatedly delayed by disagreements with the producers, the writer, the extras, and others.

Even on the best days, when Bruce was in good spirits, the weather was good, the extras showed up on time, the praying mantises behaved themselves, and everything else seemed to be going smoothly, the problems of working with a part-American, part-Chinese crew, not to mention a cameraman who spoke nothing but Japanese, considerably slowed production progress. To top things off, the extras that were needed for the mass fight scenes were mostly members of rival gangs and "families" of street fighters. When they were unleashed in front of the camera, they often abandoned all their instructions and engaged in bloody free-form mayhem. The director's cry of "Cut!" had little effect, and many of the fight scenes had to be drastically modified to be included in the final movie. I can only imagine what chaos this must have been, and how Bruce, who despised street fighting, must have recoiled at these scenes.

Then there were the accidents. Bruce and Bob Wall squared off in one scene, in which Wall, playing the main villain, Oharra, breaks off two bottles and threatens Bruce. Bruce knocks Wall over by using his hands to throw prearranged, lightning-fast punches and kicks. Unfortunately, in the filmed take, as I understand it, there was a problem that resulted in the glass bottle cutting Bruce's hand. Blood spurted everywhere, and Bruce was hurt badly enough to require twelve stitches.

This accident set the schedule back by a week. In another scene, Bruce had to slip by a cobra, but the cobra struck and bit him before he could get by. Luckily, the snake had been de-venomed, but Bruce was out of action with the painful bite for a day or two. What's more, one of the extras nearly drowned in the South China Sea when the water turned rough during a filming session shot from a boat.

The producer and director had to adapt to Hong Kong methods of filmmaking: the script was considered to be infinitely elastic, changeable according to circumstances and the whims of the director, stars and crew; all sound had to be dubbed after the film was shot, because of the background noise from the surrounding city; the Chinese crew was used to making all edits and cuts in the camera as the film was being shot, to save money, rather than editing in an editing room; and the physical resources, such as props and sets, were largely improvised on a shoestring budget. The idea of continuity was considered an expensive luxury. But, in the end, the film was wrapped, and the post-production started at Golden Harvest. I must say hearing all of this made me wonder if I really wanted to do a movie, if it's all worth it. Of course, I decided it was.

Chapter Fifteen

Goodbye My Friend

"I was one of the last people Bruce talked to over the phone. He called and told me that he fought to have the director put my name as the top billing of my movie...Then the next day came the news that he was dead!"
—Jhoon Rhee

At this time, Bruce had lost some weight during the filming, due to the heat, humidity, and his exertion. In anticipation of the profits from "Enter the Dragon," Bruce splurged—partly, I imagine, to make himself feel better—and ordered a gold Rolls Royce Corniche. Sadly, he wouldn't live to receive it. On May 10, 1973, Bruce was working in the sound editing room at Golden Harvest, dubbing sound on the final print of the movie. It was a very hot, humid day, typical in monsoon season, but the air conditioning had been shut off to keep it from interfering with the recording. The dubbing room was very hot and still, and, as I understand it, Bruce had been working for some time. He had excused himself to go to the rest room, and when he got there, he collapsed on the floor, although he didn't lose consciousness. When he returned to the dubbing room, he collapsed and passed out. He began to vomit and convulse.

The crew rushed Bruce to a hospital, where he continued to have convulsions, and seemed to have trouble breathing. He ran a fever, shook, and didn't respond to stimuli. The doctors stood by, ready to perform a tracheotomy if necessary, while Bruce was examined by a neurosurgeon. The neurosurgeon correctly diagnosed a swelling of the brain, and Bruce was given a drug called Manitol to reduce the swelling. The results were dramatic. Soon, Bruce was able to control his movements a little, then he opened his eyes; then, still unable to speak, he made signs with his hands. After a while, he could speak, although his words were slurred. By the time he was transferred to another hospital, he could use his memory and, as was typical of him, joke about his situation. None of the doctors had any idea what had caused Bruce's collapse, or his subsequent symptoms; the doctors were agreed, however, that my friend had been very close to death. When I heard of this episode, I was very troubled, of course, but then I thought Bruce would bounce back as strong as ever. After all, he was Bruce Lee.

Later examinations in Los Angeles, which included an electroencephalogram and a complete physical, turned up nothing; the doctors told Bruce and Linda that he had the body of an 18-year old. They told the Lees that the collapse was caused by a cerebral edema, a buildup of fluid around the brain, but that its cause was a mystery. Though there was no sign of epilepsy, Bruce was prescribed Dilantin, a standard anti-seizure drug.

While Bruce was in Los Angeles, he agreed to a schedule of promotional events for "Enter the Dragon," which included an appearance on "The Tonight Show." He decided that he and his family should return to the United States, and that his film career should begin to move away from the action pictures he had been known for. He felt that the craze for kung-fu pictures would peak with "Enter the Dragon," and then would begin to wane. He wanted to become a serious actor. His timing was right; six- and seven-figure offers were arriving in a steady stream from around the world. His earlier written goal of earning $10 million by 1980 appeared to be not only possible but inevitable. Everything was going his way.

Shortly before the release of "Enter the Dragon," Bruce decided to try to finish up "Game of Death," which so far only consisted of the fight sequences he had shot the year before. He consulted with Raymond Chow, and they began work on a script, and on casting the remainder of the film.

In early summer, Bruce came to Hong Kong to help me finish my movie, "The Sting of the Dragon Master" (a.k.a., "When Taekwondo

Strikes"). We went out to eat at some of the city's great restaurants, including a Korean establishment, and of course we'd talk and talk, eat spicy food and talk some more. We hadn't seen each other much in the last couple of years so we had a lot to talk about.

Linda recently told a friend of mine about what it was like to dine out with Bruce and me. "The conversation was nonstop," she said. "Jhoon had just made a film and Bruce had laid the groundwork for that. So they talked at great length about the movie industry, and whether Jhoon could be a part of that because of his martial arts ability. They'd talk about the karate world in the United States. And they'd eat. You know, Korean food—thinly sliced meats, kim chee, pickles, fish and veggies— can be pretty spicy. Bruce did not always eat spicy food but he loved it, and seemed to eat it whenever Jhoon was around. I remember when we ate that food, Bruce would be sweating and sweating and loving it."

180

One time in Hong Kong we went to lunch—it was the last time I'd ever see Bruce—and on the way home, he drove very reck-lessly. So I said to him, "Bruce, I have some advice I want to give you. First, you must understand that you are a living legend. One out of ten-million people could accomplish what you have accomplished. Don't take chances—drive more carefully. And, take care of yourself." He sort of laughed it off and said, "Jhoon, you are always too serious."

On July 20, 1973, Bruce met with Chow at Bruce's home to talk about the film, then the two of them drove to the home of Betty Ting-pei, an actress they had cast in the film. They talked and then Chow left in the early evening, but made plans to meet Bruce and Ting-pei later for dinner. Bruce complained of a headache, and Ting-pei gave him a tablet of Equagesic, a prescription pain reliever. The two continued to talk, and then Bruce said that he didn't feel well. He went to lie down in a bedroom, and fell asleep. Chow called later to find out where they were, and Ting-pei told him that she couldn't get Bruce to wake up.

Chow returned to the apartment and tried to wake Bruce, but couldn't get any response. He had Ting-pei call a doctor, who spent ten minutes trying to revive Bruce before calling an ambulance. Bruce was rushed to the hospital, where a team of doctors worked to revive him, but it was no use. Linda was at the hospital when the ambulance arrived, but it was too late: Bruce Lee was pronounced dead on arrival at age 32, a month before the release of his first U.S. film.

181

I was one of the last people Bruce talked to over the phone. He called and told me that he fought to have the director put my name as the top billing of my movie. I thanked him for caring about me and for his efforts. Then the next day came the news that he was dead! At first, I couldn't believe it. Then as it started to sink in, I just felt devastated.

Of course, so too were many others. Recently, I mentioned Bruce to U.S. Congressman Jesse Jackson, Jr., who was eight years old at the time of Bruce's death, and had seen at least one of Bruce's movies. "When I heard on the radio that Bruce Lee died, I was very depressed," he told me. "It was the saddest day of my life."

Most readers know that Bruce's death was the subject of much speculation. There was an uproar in the Hong Kong press. Many theories were proposed to explain why a relatively young man in superb physical condition should go into a coma and die unexpectedly. The autopsy and inquest that were held showed that the edema that he had suffered earlier had returned, this time fatally. While no damage to any other organ was found, Bruce's brain was greatly swollen. The eventual verdict of "death by misadventure" rested on the scientific evidence that what ultimately killed my friend was an allergic reaction to either meprobamate or aspirin, the components of the Equagesic he had taken. While some want a mystery to surround Bruce's death, I'm convinced, as are many others, that my friend died from an edema.

Two funerals were held, one in Hong Kong for Bruce's family, friends and fans, and one in Seattle, where his body was buried. Linda Lee decided that she would bury Bruce in the place where he had found the most peace, The Emerald City.

"Enter the Dragon" broke all the international box office records set by Bruce's previous films. It was not quite as successful in Hong Kong as its predecessors, but it was unquestionably the film that set the standard for every action movie that has followed. And, true to Bruce's predictions, it made him an international superstar.

To this day, fresh flowers appear on Bruce's grave nearly every day.

What He Did, What He Could Have Done

What Bruce achieved in such a short span of time was truly remarkable. He was an incredible martial artist, an inspiring teacher, a dynamic actor, a loving father and husband, a generous friend and a truly wonderful person.

183

Someone asked me recently what I thought Bruce would have done had he not died so tragically young. I think he would have kept on making movies. He knew what audiences wanted because he was very savvy. Had Bruce lived, I think martial arts today would be three times larger in popularity. But I also think Bruce would have explored non-martial arts movie roles, as well. Joe Lewis, who later starred in two martial arts films, believes Bruce would have explored comedic roles as well. His wit and sense of humor were natural gifts, and are strikingly apparent in certain action scenes throughout his films. He had that magnetic presence that captivates the viewer. I recently joined together with some superb business people to start a multimedia company and launched a web site, JhoonRhee.com. If Bruce were alive I'm sure he would have created a web site before I did; he was so popular, so energetic, such a risk-taker, and so committed to excellence and new ideas. For sure, he would have given me suggestions for my site, and he'd be happy for me and the success I've achieved. In fact, if Bruce were still alive, JhoonRhee.com would probably be only the second most popular martial arts and fitness site on the Internet, rather than number one!

Yes, Bruce would have encouraged and congratulated me, but he also would have teased me. He once really got me with one of his gags. We were talking very seriously about health and nutrition, and I wondered out loud just how healthy I was. Bruce looked at me with some concern and said he knew of a simple test that measures one's health. "Let's see how healthy you are, Jhoon," he said. He took a dime out of his pocket and pressed it hard onto my forehead. He said, "Now bend over and smack the back of your head until the dime falls off." Thinking this was some sort of ancient Chinese practice, rooted in years of time-tested tradition, I did as told. I hit the back of my head. But the dime didn't come off. Bruce said, "Good. Now do it again, harder this time." I really smacked myself. Again! And again! But still the dime didn't fall. Bruce said, "Oh Jhoon, you are really healthy. But what happened to the dime?" I felt my forehead and found no coin. Bruce started laughing and laughing! He then held up the

184

dime. You see, when he pressed it against my forehead, he numbed my skin, making it feel as if a dime really were stuck there. Bruce, of course, had used sleight of hand to remove the dime without my seeing it. I've used that trick—several times since then. And I still laugh at how silly I must have looked to Bruce that day so long ago.

On a more serious note, I think it is important to keep Bruce's legacy alive, so that future generations can get to know the man and his art. Naturally, I am not alone. All of Bruce's friends in the martial arts world do what they can to remind people of Bruce's kind heart, keen intellect and incredible physical abilities. Linda, who has remarried and is now Linda Lee Cadwell, is of course the champion of Bruce's legacy. She helped to establish the Bruce Lee Educational Foundation, a nonprofit organization whose goal is to preserve and perpetuate the work of Bruce Lee and to educate all interested parties about the art and philosophy of this extraordinary man. The foundation's web site is www.bruceleefoundation.com.

185

Linda in 1993 endowed the Bruce Lee Scholarship Fund through the U.S. Pan Asian-American Chamber of Commerce, whereby a deserving Asian-American student receives the "Excellence 2000 Award" in his honor. This Bruce Lee scholarship is given annually "to that student who exhibits a strong character, and who has persevered and prevailed over adversity."

On the 25th anniversary of Bruce's death, Linda delivered a eulogy to her late husband to a group of family and friends who had gathered at the Seattle cemetery where Bruce is buried. It was the same one she delivered 25 years earlier. She said: "If you believe as I do that energy never disappears, but is merely transformed, then the energy that was Bruce continues to revitalize our spirits, unceasingly urging us to realize our talents through the path of self-knowledge."[37]

I, too, believe in that energy and feel that Bruce's short life shaped mine in so many ways. My memory of him is one of several motivating forces in my life, and I plan on living a healthy, happy and long life. In the 1970s, I saw a "60 Minutes" program in which a 109-year-old man was bathing in a creek. When asked what he was doing, he said, "I'm cleaning up for my mother's birthday party!" His mother turned 135 years old that day and was featured as the world's oldest living person. This is when I changed one of my goals. I had wanted to live to be 120, but after seeing this show I now set my sight on 136, to break the longevity record! Of course, I need to find out whether she lived past her 135th year to know just how long I need to live!

Before then, however, I have other plans. For instance, I have invited a large number of people, including the entire U.S. Congress, to attend my 100th birthday. During my birthday party I will perform for my guests 100 push-ups and hope that other guests join me—

[37]Linda Tagliaferro, Bruce Lee, Lerner Publications Co., Minneapolis, Minn., 2000.

no matter what their age is. Linda recently wrote me to RSVP for her and her family. "Please reserve a seat for us at your 100th birthday party on January 7, 2032. We feel sure we will all make it."

I only wish Bruce Lee could be there with all of us; he and I would do a martial arts demonstration together! And afterwards go out together, eat some spicy Korean food, and talk into the night about how we're going to use martial arts as a means to serve society and advance the cause of human happiness. Bruce certainly will be with us in our hearts and minds—as he always is. Because of his extraordinary spirit and character, I am forever grateful to this man. His many gifts of excellence affected my life. Bruce Lee, just being who he was, helped me be a better man…and the world a better place. I sure do miss him.

187

Epilogue

The Dragon's Script:
A Graphologist
Looks At Bruce Lee

Editor's Note

Much has been written about Bruce Lee, including this most recent authoritative memoir by his good friend and fellow martial artist, Jhoon Rhee. The Bruce Lee legend has been told and retold in books and movies alike. Though we know him best through his movies such as "Enter the Dragon" and "Fist of Fury," we know that we don't know everything, nor can we about this great man. We know that he was fully human, and we know that his name and image will likely live on forever among the great masters.

In order to complement Jhoon Rhee's intimate portrait of Bruce Lee from the perspective of one martial artist and philosopher to another, MVM (Multimedia Vertical Markets) Books specially commissioned Koshu Morioka-sensei, Japan's leading graphologist as well as a master teacher of brush calligraphy, to analyze the handwriting of Bruce Lee. Like the voice and the image from the screen, Bruce Lee's handwriting provides traces left by the living legend himself.

Here then is Morioka-sensei's insightful analysis of Bruce Lee, the man, which reveals what one master sees in the pen strokes of another. This is the first time for any of Morioka-sensei's hand-writing analysis to appear in print in English. The translation is by William Reed, MVM News Bureau Chief in Japan. Special thanks to Linda Lee Cadwell, wife of the late Bruce Lee; as well as to Grandmaster Jhoon Rhee, for sharing a copy of a hand-written letter personally written to Master Rhee by Bruce Lee.

Japanese commentary (clockwise from to bottom)

1) Right-slant—orthodox type
2) Collapsed spaces—physical or mental distress
3) Long right-stroke extension—passion and zeal
4) Large enclosure—standing above the crowd
5) Long horizontal starting stroke—genius and exceptional talent

Explanation:

A "collapsed space" is any enclosed loop such as a handwritten "e" or "a" which is so small that there is no white space in the loop.

A "large enclosure" is a curved stroke enclosing or engulfing more space than is typical, or than is required to write that character, such as a "g" or "y" with a large looping tail..

古伝型
オーソドックスなタイプ

From a martial artist with a screwed up back but who has discove. a new powerful kick!

字中きれ
つぶれあり.

心身のどこ
かに若い
初芽が
ありそう.

横線左方長差生型
才気のひらめきとみ

たばらい気
熱中する性格

大孤型
手の上だけない

大物の相

Handwriting Analysis

191

Bruce Lee's handwriting demonstrates the following characteristics:

A person born to greatness, though more inclined to an orthodox approach than to eccentricity. Faithfully adheres to the fundamentals, and passionately pursues them in action. Exceptional skill, with a superb sense of balance. Capable of delivering strong power in momentary bursts of energy, yet tempering this power with a high degree of self-control. Able to release energy with natural grace. Quiet on the surface, but splendid in action.

Financially fortunate. Dominant toward the opposite sex, and not likely to be compatible with a type who is similarly strong-willed. Signs of physical distress which could have an impact on health. Exceptional athletic ability and physical energy.

As cited above, Bruce had the ability to release power in bursts of energy with, at the same time, strong self-control. Significantly, the presence of these conflicting forces can create strong internal stress over time, worthy of medical attention.

Morioka-sensei has published widely in Japan and regularly appears on nationwide television programs such as Warate iitomo. He is also the founder of SOGEIKAI School of Calligraphy, with students numbering in the thousands. His client list for Graphology, the art of Handwriting Analysis, includes the Tokyo Metropolitan Police Department, as well presidents of Japanese corporations. Morioka-sensei's ability to read character in the strokes of a person's hand or brush writing is close to magic, but soundly grounded in the principles of Depth Psychology, in which he specialized as a graduaute of the Psychology Department of Japan's leading institution of higher learning, Tokyo University.

Appendix

Bruce Lee Educational Foundation

The Foundation welcomes members, who receive the exclusive quarterly newsletter for members only, the Foundation handbook, patch, and notification of and reduced-fee admission to annual and regional seminars. The Foundation, a 501-C3 non-profit organization, accepts tax-deductible gifts. For information contact:

The Bruce Lee Educational Foundation
PO Box 1390
Clovis, CA 93613
www.bruceleefoundation.com
559 298-5553 (phone and fax)
email: jfjkdinfo@aol.com

The Bruce Lee Story

The Bruce Lee Story, by Linda Lee, is available through:

Ohara Publications
24715 Rockefeller Ave.
P.O. Box 918
Santa Clarita, CA   91380
1-800-423-2874

The Bruce Lee and Jhoon Rhee Legacy in the United States

By the Associated Press and The Washington Post

Bruce Lee and Jhoon Rhee enjoyed a unique friendship over the course of ten years until Bruce Lee's death in 1973. They spent countless hours talking "into the night about how we're going to use martial arts as a means to serve society and advance the cause of human happiness."

The following account written by the "Associated Press" and printed in "The Washington Post," chronicles the success of these two men—along with numerous other people—in developing the martial arts into a popular mass-market sport activity in the United States and throughout the world. The martial arts movies referred to in the seventh paragraph were dominated by Bruce Lee, who did the most to popularize martial arts through television and film.

Karate had the head start, but the Japanese martial art is getting outmuscled in the marketplace by a relative newcomer, Korean taekwondo.

Even leaders of karate organizations concede that the Korean immigrants who have been opening taekwondo schools are creating a growing business.

"I think taekwondo is better marketed and better organized and is on its way to becoming larger than karate," said Jo Mirza, martial arts chairman of the American Athletic Union and president of the AAU's karate section.

The two martial arts look similar. Both employ many

of the same moves, although karate has more punching while taekwondo puts more emphasis on kicking, said George E. Anderson, president of the USA Karate Federation, a separate karate group.

For many Americans who are considering starting a martial art, the difference is blurred, Mirza said. "They are being brought in for karate and taught taekwondo or vice versa," he said. The terms are sometimes even used interchangeably.

Up to 10 million people are involved in karate and probably an equal number are in taekwondo, Anderson said.

Karate arrived in America earlier, brought over after World War II by U.S. soldiers who served in Japan. Taekwondo began its growth in the 1960s. Both benefited from the martial arts movie hits of the early 1970s.

A combination of karate conservatism and Korean hustle seems to have accounted for taekwondo's surge, the experts say. Karate organizers didn't work together as well to develop public interest, Mirza said.

"Koreans are very sharp businessmen, and they collaborated," Anderson said. "They made sure the beginning gyms were highly supported. If there was an area where there was no school, they would bring a guy in and handle his money until he was successful." And a leader in this was Washington area taekwondo pioneer Jhoon Rhee, Anderson said.

Rhee arrived in the United States in the mid-1950s and toured the United States, giving seminars and helping Koreans set up their businesses.

To allay concerns that people could get hurt, he developed padding specifically for the martial art, Rhee said. Protective padding let parents feel taekwondo was safe for their children, which allowed the activity to expand, Rhee said.

Parents also wanted their children to develop discipline and respect for authority, so Rhee emphasized this in his training. "We are providing values to the kids," he said.

November 5, 1996

JhoonRhee.com

In March 2000, Grandmaster Jhoon Rhee launched what in 45 days became the world's most popular martial arts community on the Internet at www.jhoonrhee.com, according to the top 100,000 ranking by Alexa Internet, the authoritative independent rating company. By early September 2000, JhoonRhee.com achieved elite status as one of the top 10,000 sites among an estimated 9 million or so sites worldwide. The Web community's parent company, Multimedia Vertical Markets, also established the MVM News Service, which provides original coverage and timely information on martial arts worldwide.

The Internet-based community of martial arts practitioners and enthusiasts seeks to remain true to the vision and ideals that Bruce Lee and Jhoon Rhee pursued together with passion beginning more than 40 years ago. JhoonRhee.com and its associated Web sites therefore follow the natural extension of martial arts into fitness, the healing arts, success sciences, and character development.

Membership in the JhoonRhee.com community brings access to many services at no charge. These include:

RheeMail:	email
RheeNet:	Dial up Internet access
RheeOrganizer:	A powerful, personal calendar
RheeSearch:	The most complete martial arts search engine on the Internet

MVM News Service: News and information on martial arts, fitness, and the healing arts from correspondents worldwide.

Tournament Coverage: Timely and complete coverage of martial arts tournaments worldwide.

Other MVM community sites:

Martial Arts:

Aikido2000.com
Judo2000.com
Karate2000.net
Kungfu2000.com
Taichi2000.com
Taekwondo2000.com

Fitness, Healing Arts, Personal Growth:

Fit for Life
Simple Truths
Healing Arts
Joy of Discipline

The Joy of Discipline Program

Jhoon Rhee's Joy of Discipline before-and-after school program uses taekwondo as a vehicle for children's character education. During the nine-week program, children gain an experience of personal accomplishment through self-discipline. An old Korean proverb says, "It takes a year to harvest a crop, ten years to see the full beauty of a tree, and fifty years to make a person." The Joy of Discipline Program seeks to provide a strong root for a lifetime of positive, personal growth.

A sample of testimonials follows, from both parents and educators whose children and students have participated in the Joy of Discipline—and from a child, Hana, who kept a journal about her classes (available in its entirety under "Joy of Discipline" at www.jhoonrhee.com).

"I wanted to take this opportunity to thank you for your hard work and dedication to our students at Hutchison. The Joy of Discipline Program has not only benefited the children, but also provided parents with the opportunity to participate in an after-school activity with their children. It is inspirational to observe children and adults learning together. I am hopeful that the respect and self-control you impress on these young children will remain with them and guide them through their lives."

Jacqueline Cheshire, PTA President
Herndon, VA

"I want you to know how valuable your program, "The Joy of Discipline," has been to our son, Jacob, and to his parents. Jacob is a boy who is advanced in his studies, but like some kids, is relatively slower at sports and physical development. Through your class twice a week over a very brief 10 weeks from February through May, Marilyn and I have seen a dramatic improvement in his skills and physical development. The improvement was not just in his learning the 14-step karate form, but in his general ability to take instructions, to increase his performance by carrying them out, and to understand personal performance and meditation. When I attended your class, I was very favorably impressed by the mastery you had over the more than 20 kids from ages 5 to 12. Also, I found your program extremely well designed to teach individual and community values, and effectively communicate them to the kids...

"I was particularly impressed with the performance and progress you were able to make with some of the other kids who we know from Jacob's class who have had some behavioral problems in school, and with some who did not initially appear very coordinated."

John Moore
Father of Jacob Moore, 7 years old
Northern Virginia

"Thank you for bringing the Joy of Discipline Program to Rose Hill School. In the few months that you have worked with our students, I have been pleased with the results.

"First, and most important, the children have learned many positive values through your efforts. Patience, diligence and respect for themselves and others are reflected in all your lessons. This thoroughly supports the attention to character development provided by our staff and parents. In a few cases, your influence has been profound and has gone beyond what we have been able to do. You have given these children clear, rigorous expectations, measurable success and the motivation to learn something difficult.

"In addition to the benefits to the children, I appreciate the ways in which you have welcomed our staff and made yourself available to me and to teachers. In this way, we learned about your program and you learned about our school and students. I am delighted with your willingness to provide resources and training for the adults in our community as well.

"Finally, the response from parents has been overwhelmingly positive. The final session, during which families viewed what the children learned, was most impressive. The opportunity to listen to Master Rhee added to the impact of the occasion.

"Thank you for your commitment to our students and for the excellent quality of your work with them. I look forward to continuing this relationship and appreciate the many benefits it brings to our children and community."

Sincerely,
Marcy Mager, Principal
Alexandria, VA

"I am writing to express my sincerest appreciation for all you have done for the students of Clearview Elementary who are involved in the Joy of Discipline Program. Over the course of the year I have observed a

201

significant change in the positive attitudes displayed by each of the students.

"As a parent, I am also impressed at how well the confidence, discipline, and self control you instill carries beyond your classroom. I have noticed a positive change in my son's behavior both at home and at school since he began this program in September.

"I am also pleased with the way you stress alternative means for handling conflict and peer pressure. These kids now have the ability to make good choices about their safety, as well as others' when faced with a difficult or potentially physical situation.

"I enjoyed participating in your program, as well…It gives parents an opportunity to learn something new along with their child…is an excellent form of physical fitness [and] I feel that my confidence has improved relative to my ability to defend myself if necessary. As a professional woman, I often have to travel alone on business to different cities and am glad that I know my options should I ever find myself in a compromising situation."

Joan Wirth
Herndon, VA

"I want to thank you for all you have done for Becky and Katie. And I want to let you know that you really have taught me a lot—"My 4 Daily Affirmations"—I will never forget. And I hope the girls won't either. You are a wonderful human being to work with these kids and this program. It's not the martial arts—it is the words, the wis-

dom, the confidence that you share with these children—
and their parents. I wish you the very, very best—now
and always. God will bless you for the gifts you have
given these children."

Thank you always!
Lynne Gagnon
Northern Virginia

"My son Michael has participated in the Joy of Discipline
Program since last year. His experience with the program
has been wonderful, and slowly I believe he is developing
the self-control he needs to have a rewarding and successful experience in school. We try to reinforce the things
he learns by using them at home and in other activities
outside of the school. Most importantly, I see these
advances and he does not even realize that the program is
doing this for him. He believes he is just having fun.
Thank you for your dedication to our children."

Janice Pritchett
Alexandria, VA

"As parents of two young daughters, we feel strongly
about instilling strong values in them. We look for programs which will assist us in teaching discipline, self-
respect and the respect of others….Emily, our first grader,
has been a participant in your Joy of Discipline Program.
While she has not mastered all the kicks and punches and
blocks, she has gained in less obvious ways, such as self-
control, team spirit and confidence. We applaud your
efforts to bring this program into the schools directly to

the students, where it can do so much good. All the elements of your program are best learned as early as possible if children are to become leaders."

Jim and Brenda Swain
Alexandria, VA

"Joy of Discipline: Viewpoint of a Child"
By Hana Slevin, 4th Grade
Northern Virginia

"Class 4: Tonight I was so excited to go to the Joy of Discipline because after the wonderful class on Monday, as soon as I left the building I wished I were back there again! Now tonight, I finally was!

"We started off with our "student creed." It goes like this: 'To build true confidence through knowledge in the mind, honesty in the heart, and strength in the body.' Then we had our welcome bow. It's actually fun to say all of those words! Then we practiced our Kamsah form, meaning Appreciation, which is 10 basic steps. Mr. Carlson said that we were going to have a contest between the girls and the boys for the Kamsah form! We had the girls in a line in the back and the boys in a line in the front. Everyone in the girls' line and everyone in the boys' line had a turn as a leader as we practiced the basic form. Then we had the contest! First, the boys all performed the form, and then the girls did. Mr. Carlson said that it was a tie. I agreed! We both said the steps with the same loudness and we both stayed together when we performed the steps in a straight line, and they were both great! So we each got two points for the star contest!

"Next, Mr. Carlson had us all move back to the end of the room and had one of the parents hold up a board next to the wall. Mr. Carlson said that he was about to demonstrate the confidence that we need to break a board. Breaking a board isn't just the strength, power, and ability that you have to break the board, but it represents thinking, concentration, true power and knowledge in your head, and confidence inside yourself. I knew what he was explaining. The tradition of breaking a board wasn't just a tradition, it represented true confidence in yourself. You need the confidence and courage to break it, and look at the positive things, and not the negative.

"Then Mr. Carlson backed up, ran and jumped off the wall, then aimed for the board and missed! Then he backed up again and ran up to the wall again and broke the board into many pieces! I was amazed. And without him telling me, I knew that what he meant by missing and trying again, was not giving up, and that you always have to try your very best to get where you want to be in life.

"Then it was the end of the lesson. The lesson seemed shorter than it really was, but I definitely knew that I had learned a lot today. In a mere 45 minutes, I had learned almost a lifetime's worth. I had the most wonderful time tonight at the Joy of Discipline, and I really look forward to the next lesson on Monday."

"Class 12: This evening at the Joy of Discipline, we had our tournament! I didn't know what we were going to be doing in the tournament until tonight, when Mr. Carlson told us. What we were doing was using the reactors for self-defense (blocking), and a fencing-type thing ("battling"), as you might be able to call it but it's not exactly "battling." We had done this at the beginning of this Joy of Discipline year. Only a few people got to do it back at the beginning of the year. I was one of them.

"There were five rounds to this tournament. Every time that you touched the other person with the reactors, Mr. Carlson would say, "Stop." Then the judges would say if they saw it or not. In order for that person to receive the point, at least three of the judges had to agree with the hit. Patty and I were the first two up. We went against each other. It was difficult to battle a friend, knowing that either way, one of us would or would not go on to the next round. I won the first round.

"I lost my 'winning streak' in the end of the third round. I got the most beautiful bronze medal with an awesome martial arts picture on it that hung on a red, white and blue ribbon! Everyone got a beautiful medal (silver, yellow, or bronze) of some kind. Each one of us had a wonderful time.

"I was very proud of myself and everybody today. The Joy of Discipline is a great part of my life!"

The Joy of Discipline Program, beginning in 2001, intends to expand from its roots in the Washington, D.C. metropolitan area. For information, contact MVM at 703 263-9505.

U.S. Congressional Record Tribute to Jhoon Rhee,

April 11, 2000

By the Hon. Nick Smith of Michigan, U.S. Representative

Mr. Speaker, it is my honor today to recognize a great American on the occasion of his recent selection by the National Immigrant Forum, in conjunction with the Immigration and Naturalization Service, as one of 200 most famous American immigrants of all time: Grandmaster Jhoon Goo Rhee.

Master Rhee, who shares the honor with such American icons as Albert Einstein, Hyman Rickover and Knute Rockne, is the sole immigrant of Korean ancestry to make the list. Well known as one of the world's foremost authorities on the martial arts and recognized as the father of taekwondo in the United States, Grand Master Rhee has established himself as more than just a famous instructor. But his road to success and achieving the American dream wasn't easy, nor would he have wanted it that way.

When Jhoon Rhee came to the United States in 1956, he spoke little English and had less money--$46 to be exact. Still, he enrolled at Southwest Texas State Teachers College in San Marcos determined to create a better life for himself. Although at first it took him a half-hour to read one page of text, he became increasingly proficient in English through discipline and perseverance, traits that for decades he has so eloquently translated from the martial arts for people from all walks of life.

Those traits also are the core of his action philosophy, a philosophy grounded in the principles of the martial arts, but applicable to everyone. It calls for people to build confidence through knowledge in the mind, honesty in the heart and strength in the body, and then to lead by example.

Leading by example is exactly what Master Rhee does. Despite his 68 years, each day as part of his daily stretching and meditation regimen, he does 1,000 push-ups and 1,000 sit-ups. Not even the fittest 20 year-old can match those feats. But the discipline, determination and perseverance involved are life lessons that far transcend martial arts and athleticism. He has enabled people everywhere to realize their potential and apply themselves successfully to whatever it is they set themselves to do. It's the philosophy Master Rhee embraced so long ago and which has stood the test of time—the same philosophy which took him from someone who barely could speak the language of his new country, to one of the world's most sought-after motivational speakers.

There is no dream too large for Grandmaster Rhee, but I'm sure even he has difficulty comprehending how many millions of people around the world owe their positive, constructive ways of living to his wholesome influences.

Many of our colleagues, Mr. Speaker, know first hand Master Rhee's call to realize the aspects of life larger than self. We know this because he founded the U.S. Congressional Taekwondo Club and has taught more than 250 current or former Members of Congress not only the art of taekwondo, but also the art of living a healthier and happier life. We know the affection he engenders to all who make his acquaintance, whether through athletics, business or when hearing his motivational presentation.

Master Rhee's success is wide ranging. Aside from his accomplishments in taekwondo and in training world-class athletes, he has starred in feature films, authored a number of books, served as a goodwill ambassador and started a hugely successful business venture. He also is held in the highest regard as an innovator and teacher.

But perhaps where he excels most is in an area that is missing so dearly in today's world—the role of husband, father and citizen. Jhoon Rhee deports himself with the utmost respect and dignity for those with whom he deals and with society in general. For more than 50 years, he has embraced the role model aspect of a life that comes with international renown, a role taken for granted by so many and perfected by so few. He gladly accepts the responsibility of presenting himself and his way of life as an emblem to be worn proudly.

This is not just my assessment. His contributions to buttress America's culture with pride and decorum are echoed by many distinguished citizens in and out of government. Among his biggest fans are boxing legend Muhammad Ali, Parade magazine Publisher Walter Anderson and motivational speaker Tony Robbins. Jack Valenti of the Motion Picture Association of America has said, 'Master Rhee defies the assumed rush of years. He is an ageless patriot, whose brand of unbreakable loyalty is seldom seen. . . .'

Our esteemed colleague Ike Skelton says, 'Master Rhee is an American treasure.' Our esteemed former colleague Bob Livingston says it quite simply: 'Master Rhee is one of the greatest Americans I know.'

At an age when even the most industrious of people tend to enjoy the leisure of their later years, Master Rhee at age 68 continues with remarkable energy to exert his positive influence on people of all ages throughout the country and the globe. He has recently launched a new global project, the JhoonRhee.com Web site, where he continues to promote the martial arts, fitness, the healing arts and a way of life whereby, in his words, 'Everybody is happy with every breath of life.'

On March 17, 1992, President George Bush named Master Rhee one of his Daily Points of Light. President Bush said, 'The true measure of any individual is found in the way he or she treats others—and the person who regards others with love, respect and charity holds a priceless treasure in his heart….any definition of a successful life must include others. Your efforts provide a shining example of this standard.'

Master Rhee's devotion to the principles of America's Founding Fathers is unsurpassed. He instills in his countrymen the Founders' vision and demonstrates the power of that vision to people throughout the world to show them the path to freedom, peace and prosperity. He understands that everyone on this planet has the right to be happy. But to achieve that happiness, individuals must accept the foundation of perfect human character that entails exercising true freedom approved by one's conscience, and never to practice false freedom licensed by selfishness.

Master Rhee is a proud American who cherishes the words freedom, free enterprise, democracy and heritage. He lives the American Dream. Indeed, he exemplifies it. He inspires all, and with a special enthusiasm toward the young, to live lives of honor and integrity. The eloquence and conviction of his message to live noble lives of grand purpose penetrates the most hardened hearts and cynical souls.

His accomplishments are legion. A 10th Degree Black Belt, he introduced the martial arts to Russia in the early 1990s, where now there are 65 studios that bear his name. He is the author of five books on taekwondo, a member of the Black Belt Hall of Fame and the recipient of the National Association of Professional Martial Artists' Lifetime Achievement Award.

He was named by *Black Belt* magazine as one of the top two living martial artists of the 20th Century and also as 'Martial Arts Man of the Century' by the Washington, D.C., Touchdown Club. He has been featured on the cover of Parade, collaborated on several projects with Bruce Lee and had the lead role in the films, "When Taekwondo Strikes" and "The Silent Master." Additionally, he created and choreographed the martial arts ballet—the basis for today's popular `musical forms' competition—and invented and implemented the safety equipment used in major open tournaments, including the 2000 Olympic Games in Sydney.

I would like to summarize some of Master Rhee's accomplishments, a truly impressive list of famous firsts. He was the:

First master to teach taekwondo in America: Master Rhee introduced taekwondo to America in 1956.

First master to work out to music: Master Rhee created the Martial Arts Ballet which then gave birth to the Exercise to Music craze.

First master to invent safety equipment: Master Rhee invented martial arts safety equipment after one of his students was injured in a competition. The introduction of safety equipment enabled martial arts studios to get insurance. Because of that, parents began to send their kids to martial arts instructors, and the martial arts industry was born.

First master to promote martial arts in the U.S. through television advertising: Master Rhee produced the award-winning "Nobody Bothers Me" television commercials that helped popularize martial arts.

First master to use the color belt system: At one time, martial arts awarded only white, brown or black belts. Master Rhee introduced the color belt award system now used worldwide.

First master who also is a concert musician: Master Rhee has been the featured musician with the Washington Symphony Orchestra and with South Korean orchestras. He played classical music on the harmonica.

First master to require black belt scholastic excellence: For more than 30 years, Master Rhee has required his students to maintain a `B' average or better to qualify for a black belt.

First master to train Members of Congress in martial arts: Master Rhee founded the U.S. Congressional Taekwondo Club, where he has taught Members of Congress without interruption since 1965.

First American to open martial arts studios in the Soviet Union: Master Rhee first traveled to Moscow in 1991 to teach taekwondo and now has 65 Jhoon Rhee Do studios throughout the Commonwealth of Independent States. Learning English is a requirement for a black belt.

First to teach martial arts in America's public schools: Master Rhee launched his Joy of Discipline program of martial arts and character education in America's public schools in the early 1980s.

First taekwondo master to star in his own movies: Master Rhee starred with Angela Mao in "When Taekwondo Strikes." As Grandmaster Lee, he is the underground leader of a group of patriots in Japanese occupied Korea.

First martial artist to train a world heavyweight boxing champion: Master Rhee taught the legendary Bruce Lee his kicking techniques, and Bruce Lee taught him how to punch. Master Rhee then taught Muhammad Ali what Ali later called his powerful `Accu-punch.' Ali used it in 1976 to knock out Richard Dunn in Munich and also in the Joe Frazier heavyweight title bout.

First and only martial artist to be named "Man of the Century".

And now, Master Rhee is the first and only native Korean to be named as one of America's top 200 immigrants of all time. Mr. Speaker, the National Immigrant Forum made a wise choice. He is a man of character and the prototype role model for the new century. I can think of few others so worthy of such a designation.

Master Rhee's Patents for His Safe-T-Punch Gloves

United States Patent [19]

Rhee

[11] **3,855,633**

[45] **Dec. 24, 1974**

[54] **KARATE GLOVE**

[76] Inventor: **Jhoon Goo Rhee**, 2525 No. Ridgeview Rd., Arlington, Va. 22207

[22] Filed: **Aug. 30, 1973**

[21] Appl. No.: **393,034**

Related U.S. Application Data

[63] Continuation-in-part of Ser. No. 252,054, May 10, 1972, abandoned.

[52] **U.S. Cl.** .... **2/18, 2/161 A**
[51] **Int. Cl.** **A41d 13/08**
[58] **Field of Search** .... 2/18, 19, 20, 21, 161 R, 2/161 A, 162, 163, 165, 166, 159, 160

[56] **References Cited**
UNITED STATES PATENTS

961,149	6/1910	Maynard	2/18
2,574,086	11/1951	Broderick	2/18
2,907,047	10/1959	Steinberg	2/161
3,141,173	7/1964	Jackson et al.	2/161
3,217,332	11/1965	Gross	2/16

FOREIGN PATENTS OR APPLICATIONS

| 719,956 | 12/1954 | Great Britain | 2/18 |

Primary Examiner—Werner H. Schroeder
Attorney, Agent, or Firm—Millen, Raptes & White

[57] **ABSTRACT**

The invention relates to protective gloves useful in the art of karate, etc. The glove comprises a tough outer casing with resilient foam means therein. Various embodiments of the glove are disclosed which are adapted to protect the hand of the wearer, and also the wrist and a portion of the arm. The glove is detachably retained on the hand by various types of strap means.

9 Claims, 8 Drawing Figures

United States Patent [19]

Rhee

[11] **Patent Number:** **4,635,300**

[45] **Date of Patent:** **Jan. 13, 1987**

[54] **KARATE GLOVE**

[76] Inventor: Jhoon G. Rhee, 6210 Chillum Pl., NW., Washington, D.C. 20011

[21] Appl. No.: 714,395

[22] Filed: Mar. 21, 1985

[51] Int. Cl.^{4} A41D 13/10
[52] U.S. Cl. .... 2/16; 2/18; 2/161 A
[58] Field of Search .... 2/16, 161 A, 18

[56] **References Cited**

U.S. PATENT DOCUMENTS

3,903,546	9/1975	Rhee	2/16
3,924,272	12/1975	Alen et al.	2/16
3,945,045	3/1976	Rhee	2/16
4,062,073	12/1977	Rhee	2/16
4,287,610	9/1981	Rhee	2/18
4,290,147	9/1981	Brückner et al.	2/161 A

FOREIGN PATENT DOCUMENTS

0054949	6/1982	European Pat. Off.	2/16

Primary Examiner—Louis K. Rimrodt
Attorney, Agent, or Firm—James C. Wray

[57] **ABSTRACT**

A unitary flexible protective glove molded of a resilient material and adapted to be easily worn on the hand for use in the art of karate and the like is disclosed. The glove, when worn, covers a portion of the lower forearm, the wrist, and the hand. The portion of the glove covering the wrist and hand is substantially tubular in shape and designed to wrap around the wrist and forearm without the need of any securing means. There is a thumb pocket having on the inside a restraining strap. There is also a grip loop for the index, middle, ring and little fingers which is in close proximity to a finger padding section. The finger padding section and grip loop are held in close proximity by a bridging strap. The glove is designed to facilitate easy insertion of the hand without the need of securing straps.

5 Claims, 5 Drawing Figures

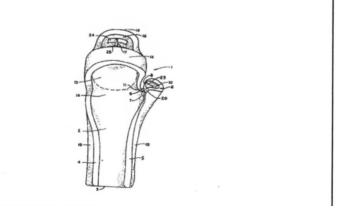

Books Available at the JhoonRhee.com
Online Store

Books by Grandmaster Jhoon Rhee

Bruce Lee and I
(MVM Books October 2000) $19.95

Chon-Ji of Tae Kwon Do Hyung
By Jhoon Rhee, et al, Paperback
(Ohara Publications 1989) $13.95

Tan-Gun and To-San of Tae Kwon Do Hyung
By Jhoon Rhee, et al, Paperback
(Ohara Publications 1989) $16.95

Won-Kyu and Yul-Kok of Tae Kwon Do Hyung
By Jhoon Rhee, et al, Paperback
(Ohara Publications 1989) $14.95

Chung-Gun and Toi Gye of Tae Kwon Do Hyung
By Jhoon Rhee, et al, Paperback
(Ohara Publications 1979) $15.95

Hwa-Rang and Chung-Mu of Tae Kwon Do Hyung
By Jhoon Rhee, et al, Paperback
(Ohara Publications 1971) $15.95

Character for Champions
By Charles Sutherland and Jhoon Rhee
2nd Printing, Revised Edition, Paperback
(MVM Books November 2000) $23.95

Books by John Corcoran

The following books by John Corcoran can be ordered at the JhoonRhee.com Web site, through your local bookstore or through certain martial arts supply companies:

The Complete Martial Arts Catalogue (1977)

The Overlook Martial Arts Dictionary (1980)

The Martial Arts: Traditions, History, People (1983)

The Martial Arts Companion (1992)

The Original Martial Arts Encyclopedia (an updated reprint of The Martial Arts: Traditions, History, People) (1993)

The Martial Arts Sourcebook (1994)

The ACMA (American Council on Martial Arts) *Instructor Certification Manual* (1998)

The Ultimate Martial Arts Q & A Book: 750 Expert Answers To Essential Questions (To be published in 2001)

Index

221